Disclaimer - Warning

This book is designed to provide helpful information on the topics covered. It is not intended to replace professional medical, health, or nutritional advice. The author and publisher make no guarantees or warranties as to the accuracy or completeness of the content within.

By using this book, you understand that any actions you take based on the information are done at your own risk. The author and publisher disclaim any liability for injuries, losses, or damages arising from the application of the ideas, techniques, or suggestions presented. Additionally, following the recipes does not guarantee the same results or success, as outcomes may vary based on individual factors. Always consult with a qualified professional before making any significant lifestyle changes.

Welcome to **The Keto Diet Cookbook**, your go-to guide for delicious, low-carb recipes that make keto easy and enjoyable that make keto easy and enjoyable!

Table of Contents

INTRODUCTION TO THE KETO DIET 1

CHAPTER ONE: DAILY MEAL RECIPES 5

- CLASSIC EGG MUFFINS 6
- AVOCADO & SALMON SALAD 6
- KETO GREEN SMOOTHIE 7
- VEGETABLE STIR-FRY WITH TOFU 7
- KETO PANCAKES 8
- GRILLED CHICKEN SALAD 8
- 5-MINUTE CHIA PUDDING 9
- KETO AVOCADO AND EGG BREAKFAST BOWL 9
- 5-MINUTE YOGURT BOWL WITH KETO TOPPINGS 10
- LOW-CARB GREEK YOGURT PARFAIT 10
- CHICKEN AVOCADO SALAD 11
- CAULIFLOWER HASH BROWNS 11
- TUNA LETTUCE WRAPS 12
- AVOCADO TOAST WITH POACHED EGG 12
- GREEK KETO SALAD BOWL 13
- OVERNIGHT OATS 13
- TURKEY & CHEESE ROLL-UPS 14
- VEGGIE OMELET 14
- CAULIFLOWER FRIED RICE MEAL PREP BOWLS 15
- BANANA PEANUT BUTTER SMOOTHIE 15
- KETO COBB SALAD 16
- BERRY AND NUTTY BREAKFAST BOWL 16
- KETO EGG SALAD WRAPS 17
- HEALTHY BREAKFAST BURRITO 17
- KETO CHICKEN CAESAR SALAD 18
- BANANA OATMEAL PANCAKES 18
- BEEF TACO SALAD BOWL 19
- SPINACH AND MUSHROOM OMELETTE 19
- SPINACH & FETA KETO QUICHE 20
- KETO BREAKFAST CASSEROLE 20
- ZUCCHINI NOODLE LASAGNA 21
- KETO BULLETPROOF COFFEE 21
- KETO MEATLOAF WITH ALMOND FLOUR 22
- KETO COTTAGE CHEESE AND BERRY BOWL 22

CHAPTER TWO: WEEKEND TREATS AND ENTERTAINING 23

- KETO WAFFLES 24
- MINI CAPRESE SKEWERS 24
- FRITTATA 25
- CLASSIC BRUSCHETTA 25
- STUFFED AVOCADO BOATS 26
- LEMON BLUEBERRY SCONES 26
- CHIA SEED PUDDING 27
- BBQ CHICKEN SLIDERS 27
- KETO PIZZA 28
- CHEESY GARLIC BREADSTICKS 28
- BURGERS WITH CAULIFLOWER BUNS 29
- STUFFED MUSHROOMS 29
- BUFFALO WINGS 30
- CHOCOLATE-DIPPED STRAWBERRIES 30
- ZUCCHINI NOODLES WITH PESTO 31
- CINNAMON SUGAR CHURROS 31
- BACON-WRAPPED JALAPEÑOS 32
- PROSCIUTTO & MELON BITES 32
- CAULIFLOWER BITES 33
- CRISPY PARMESAN ZUCCHINI FRIES 33
- SPINACH AND CHEESE STUFFED MUSHROOMS 34
- PESTO PINWHEELS 34

CHAPTER THREE: SNACKS AND ON-THE-GO OPTIONS — 35

- CHEESE CRISPS — 36
- NO-BAKE ENERGY BITES — 36
- AVOCADO DEVILED EGGS — 37
- HUMMUS & VEGGIE WRAP — 37
- ZUCCHINI CHIPS — 38
- CRISPY CHICKPEAS — 38
- NUT BUTTER ENERGY BALLS — 39
- STUFFED DATES WITH GOAT CHEESE AND ALMONDS — 39
- MINI QUICHES — 40
- HARD-BOILED EGGS WITH AVOCADO — 40
- TRAIL MIX ENERGY BARS — 41
- CUCUMBER AND SMOKED SALMON BITES — 41
- SWEET POTATO HUMMUS — 42
- TOMATO & MOZZARELLA SALAD — 42
- KETO CHOCOLATE CHIP COOKIES — 43
- BAKED SWEET POTATO CHIPS — 43
- KETO STRAWBERRY CHEESECAKE BITES — 44
- AVOCADO TOAST — 44

CHAPTER FOUR: COCKTAIL AND BEVERAGE RECIPES — 45

- KETO MARGARITA — 46
- PIÑA COLADA — 46
- KETO MOJITO — 47
- STRAWBERRY DAIQUIRI — 47
- KETO OLD FASHIONED — 48
- COSMOPOLITAN — 48
- KETO FLAVORED SPARKLING WATER — 49
- WHISKEY SOUR — 49
- KETO ICED TEA — 50
- MAI TAI — 50
- MAI TAIKETO COLD BREW COFFEE — 51
- ESPRESSO MARTINI — 51
- KETO LEMONADE — 52
- TEQUILA SUNRISE — 52
- KETO MATCHA LATTE — 53
- LONG ISLAND ICED TEA — 53
- KETO HOT CHOCOLATE — 54
- KETO BLOODY MARY — 54
- KETO CHAI TEA LATTE — 55
- KETO COLLINS — 55
- KETO VANILLA ALMOND MILK LATTE — 56
- KETO LEMONADE VODKA SPRITZER — 56

CHAPTER FIVE: DESSERTS AND SWEET TREATS QUICK DESSERTS — 57

- CHOCOLATE AVOCADO MOUSSE — 58
- NO-BAKE PEANUT BUTTER BARS — 58
- CHEESECAKE BITES — 59
- APPLE NACHOS — 59
- KETO CUPCAKE — 60
- MICROWAVE S'MORES — 60
- ALMOND FLOUR COOKIES — 61
- CARAMEL POPCORN — 61
- KETO ICE CREAM — 62
- COCONUT MACAROONS — 62
- COCONUT CHIA PUDDING — 63
- NUTELLA BANANA ROLL-UPS — 63
- VANILLA BEAN PANNA COTTA — 64
- CINNAMON APPLE CRUMBLE — 64

CHAPTER SIX: BUILDING YOUR KETO PANTRY: ESSENTIAL STAPLES FOR A LOW-CARB LIFESTYLE — 65

- KETO PANTRY LIST - ESSENTIAL KETO-FRIENDLY STAPLES — 66
- BEST FRESH FOODS FOR KETO — 67
- 30 DAYS MEAL PLAN — 68
- SHOPPING LIST — 72
- KETO DIET METRIC CONVERSION CHART — 73
- ABOUT THE AUTHOR — 74

INTRODUCTION TO THE KETO DIET

WHAT IS KETO?

The ketogenic diet (or "keto" for short) is a low-carbohydrate, high-fat diet that has gained significant popularity for its effectiveness in promoting weight loss, supporting mental clarity, and stabilizing energy levels. By drastically reducing carbohydrate intake and replacing it with healthy fats, the body enters a state called ketosis, where it burns fat for fuel instead of carbohydrates.

Unlike most diets that rely on calorie restriction, keto is primarily about shifting the body's fuel source. This metabolic shift is why many people find keto more sustainable and satisfying than other diets.

HOW IT WORKS: THE SCIENCE OF KETOSIS

In ketosis, the liver converts fat into molecules called ketones, which the body uses for energy. Here's how it works:

- **Carbohydrate Reduction:** With fewer carbs, blood sugar and insulin levels drop, reducing fat storage.
- **Fat as Fuel:** The body starts breaking down stored fat for energy, producing ketones.
- **Brain Benefits:** Ketones cross the blood-brain barrier, supplying a steady source of energy to the brain, often enhancing focus and clarity.

The result is that the body becomes highly efficient at burning fat, which is why keto has become popular for weight loss, sustained energy, and cognitive performance.
MYTH-BUSTING SECTION

Despite its popularity, there are plenty of myths surrounding keto. Let's clear up a few of the most common ones:

- Myth: Keto is all about eating bacon and cheese.

- **Reality:** Keto emphasizes healthy fats, like avocado, nuts, seeds, olive oil, and fatty fish, not just high-saturated fats.

- **Myth:** You can't have any carbs.
- **Reality:** While keto limits carbs, small amounts from low-carb vegetables, nuts, and seeds are allowed.

- **Myth:** Keto is only for short-term weight loss.
- **Reality:** Many people use keto long-term to manage health issues, energy levels, and cognitive function

- **Myth:** Keto lacks variety.
- **Reality:** Keto meals are diverse and include everything from salads to seafood and desserts.

BENEFITS AND RISKS

Like any diet, keto has its pros and cons. Here's a balanced overview.
Benefits
- **Weight Loss:** By promoting fat burning, keto can help shed body fat.
- **Increased Energy:** Ketones provide a stable, sustained energy source.
- **Enhanced Mental Clarity:** Many report improved focus and cognitive function.
- **Metabolic Health:** Keto may help regulate blood sugar and insulin, potentially benefiting those with type 2 diabetes.
- **Reduced Cravings:** A high-fat diet can lead to greater satiety, helping reduce overall calorie intake.

Risks

- **Keto Flu:** Initial side effects, like headaches and fatigue, may occur as the body adjusts.
- **Nutrient Deficiency:** Low fruit and grain intake can limit certain nutrients.

- **Gastrointestinal Issues:** Some may experience constipation or digestive discomfort.
- **Mitigation:** Staying hydrated, increasing salt intake, and ensuring fiber from vegetables can help manage these symptoms.

SCIENTIFIC BASIS

Recent studies highlight the effectiveness of the ketogenic diet for weight loss, energy, and mental clarity. For instance, a 2021 study published in *Frontiers in Nutrition* found that ketogenic diets not only support weight loss but can also help improve insulin sensitivity and cardiovascular health markers. Another study, from *Nature*, suggests that ketosis may enhance mitochondrial function, which could explain the increase in energy and cognitive benefits many people report.

HEALTH BENEFITS

- **Enhanced Focus:** Ketones provide an alternative fuel source for the brain, which may contribute to improved focus and reduced mental fog.
- **Metabolic Health Support:** By promoting blood sugar stability, keto can be especially beneficial for people with insulin resistance or metabolic syndrome.
- **Possible Neuroprotective Effects:** There is ongoing research exploring the benefits of keto for conditions like epilepsy, Alzheimer's, and Parkinson's, as ketones may support brain health.

POTENTIAL RISKS

While the benefits of keto are numerous, there are also potential risks to be mindful of:

- **Electrolyte Imbalance:** Since keto can cause the body to release more water and salt, it's important to maintain adequate levels of sodium, potassium, and magnesium.

- **Potentially Increased Cholesterol:** Some people may experience an increase in cholesterol. Regular monitoring can help identify and manage this issue.
- **Digestive Changes:** The lack of high-fiber grains and fruits can lead to constipation, so it's essential to include fiber-rich vegetables in your keto meals.

TIPS: Start gradually, and consult a healthcare professional before starting keto, especially if you have existing health concerns.

CONCLUSION

The keto diet has become a powerful approach for those seeking weight loss, improved mental clarity, and metabolic health. Like any diet, it's essential to understand how it works and to approach it with balanced information about both benefits and risks. This cookbook aims to guide you through delicious, nutritious, and sustainable keto recipes, so you can make the most of this diet while nourishing your body and mind.

In the following sections, you'll find recipes, tips, and strategies for thriving on keto. Let's dive in!

CHAPTER ONE: DAILY MEAL RECIPES

CLASSIC EGG MUFFINS
SERVINGS: MAKES 6 MUFFINS 🕐 10 MINUTES

Ingredients

- 6 large eggs
- 1/4 cup heavy cream
- Salt and pepper to taste
- 1/4 cup diced bell pepper
- 1/4 cup chopped spinach
- 1/4 cup shredded cheese (cheddar or mozzarella)
- slices of cooked bacon, crumbled (optional)

Preparation

1. Preheat oven to 375°F (190°C).
2. In a mixing bowl, whisk the eggs, heavy cream, salt, and pepper.
3. Add bell pepper, spinach, cheese, and bacon.
4. Pour mixture into a greased muffin tin, filling each cup about 2/3 full.
5. Bake for 15-18 minutes or until set and lightly golden on top.
6. Let cool slightly before removing from the muffin tin.

Nutritional Fact:

- Calories: 120
- Fat: 9g
- Protein: 7g
- Net Carbs: 1g

AVOCADO & SALMON SALAD
SERVINGS: 1 SALAD 🕐 5 MINUTES

Ingredients

- 2 cups mixed greens
- 1/2 avocado, sliced
- 4 oz smoked salmon
- 1 tbsp olive oil
- 1 tbsp lemon juice
- Salt and pepper to taste

Preparation

1. Place mixed greens in a bowl.
2. Top with avocado slices and smoked salmon.
3. Drizzle with olive oil and lemon juice.
4. Season with salt and pepper, toss lightly to coat.

Nutritional Fact:

- Calories: 250
- Fat: 22g
- Carbohydrates: 4g
- Protein: 10g

Breakfast

KETO GREEN SMOOTHIE
SERVINGS: 1 SMOOTHIE 🕐 5 MINUTES

Ingredients

- 1/2 avocado
- 1 cup unsweetened almond milk
- 1/2 cup spinach
- 1/4 cucumber, chopped
- 1 tbsp chia seeds
- Ice cubes (optional)

Instruction

1. Place all ingredients in a blender and blend until smooth.
2. Adjust thickness with ice cubes or more almond milk.

Nutritional value:

- Calories: 160
- Fat: 14g
- Protein: 3g
- Net Carbs: 2g

VEGETABLE STIR-FRY WITH TOFU
SERVINGS: 4 SERVING 🕐 20 MINUTES

Ingredients

- 1 cup firm tofu, cubed
- 1 bell pepper, sliced
- 1 cup broccoli florets
- 1 cup snow peas
- 1 medium carrot, sliced
- 2 tablespoons soy sauce
- 1 tablespoon olive oil
- 1 teaspoon sesame oil
- 1 clove garlic, minced
- 1 teaspoon grated ginger

Instruction

1. Heat olive oil in a large skillet over medium heat. Add garlic and ginger, sauté for 1 minute.
2. Add tofu and cook until lightly browned on all sides.
3. Add vegetables and stir-fry for 5-7 minutes until tender-crisp.
4. Stir in soy sauce and sesame oil.
5. Serve warm over rice or quinoa.

Nutritional value:

- Calories: 180
- Protein: 10g
- Carbohydrates: 15g
- Fat: 10g

Breakfast

KETO PANCAKES

SERVINGS: 4 SMALL PANCAKES 🕐 15 MINUTES

Ingredients

- 1/2 cup almond flour
- 1/4 cup cream cheese, softened
- 2 large eggs
- 1/2 tsp baking powder
- 1/2 tsp vanilla extract
- Butter or coconut oil for cooking

Instruction

1. In a bowl, mix almond flour, cream cheese, eggs, baking powder, and vanilla extract.
2. Heat a non-stick skillet over medium heat; add butter or coconut oil.
3. Pour batter to form pancakes (2-3 inches in diameter).
4. Cook for 1-2 minutes on each side until golden brown.
5. Serve warm with sugar-free syrup or berries.

Nutritional value:

- Calories: 250
- Fat: 20g
- Protein: 10g
- Net Carbs: 4g

GRILLED CHICKEN SALAD

SERVINGS: 2 SERVING 🕐 15 MINUTES

Ingredients

- 1 large chicken breast, grilled and sliced
- 4 cups mixed greens
- 1/2 cup cherry tomatoes, halved
- 1/4 cup cucumber, sliced
- 1/4 cup shredded carrots
- 1/4 avocado, sliced
- 2 tablespoons olive oil
- 1 tablespoon balsamic vinegar
- Salt and pepper to taste

Instruction

1. Combine mixed greens, cherry tomatoes, cucumber, and shredded carrots in a large bowl.
2. Add grilled chicken and avocado.
3. Drizzle with olive oil and balsamic vinegar, and season with salt and pepper.
4. Toss gently and serve.

Nutritional value:

- Calories: 320
- Protein: 28g
- Carbohydrates: 12g
- Fat: 20g
- Fiber: 6g

Breakfast

5-MINUTE CHIA PUDDING

SERVINGS: 1 SMALL BOWL 🕐 5 MINUTES

Ingredients

- 2 tbsp chia seeds
- 1/2 cup unsweetened almond or coconut milk
- 1/4 tsp vanilla extract
- Optional toppings: nuts, unsweetened coconut flakes, or berries

Instruction

1. In a jar or small bowl, combine chia seeds, almond milk, and vanilla extract. Stir well.
2. Let sit for 5 minutes, then stir again.
3. Refrigerate for 1-2 hours (or overnight).
4. Top with keto-friendly toppings.

Nutritional value:

- Calories: 120
- Fat: 8g
- Protein: 4g
- Net Carbs: 2g

KETO AVOCADO AND EGG BREAKFAST BOWL

SERVINGS: 1 SERVING 🕐 10 MINUTES

Ingredients

- 1 ripe avocado
- 2 large eggs
- 2 slices of cooked bacon, crumbled
- 1 tbsp shredded cheddar cheese
- Salt and pepper to taste
- 1 tsp chopped chives

Instruction

1. Cut the avocado in half and remove the pit.
2. In a skillet, fry the eggs sunny-side-up or scrambled as preferred.
3. Place eggs over the avocado halves, top with crumbled bacon, cheese, salt, and pepper.
4. Garnish with chopped chives and serve immediately.

Nutritional value:

- Calories: 350 kcal
- Protein: 14g
- Carbs: 8g (Net Carbs: 3g)
- Fat: 29g
- Fiber: 5g

Breakfast

5-MINUTE YOGURT BOWL WITH KETO TOPPINGS

SERVINGS: 1 BOWL   🕐 5 MINUTES

Ingredients

- 1/2 cup plain, unsweetened Greek or coconut yogurt
- Savory: Avocado slices, chia seeds, salt, pepper
- Sweet: Raspberries, sugar-free syrup, or crushed nuts
- Optional toppings: nuts, seeds, shredded coconut, and a sprinkle of cinnamon for flavor and crunch.

Instruction

1. Scoop yogurt into a bowl.
2. Top with savory or sweet options.
3. Enjoy immediately.

Nutritional value:

- Calories: 90
- Fat: 5g
- Protein: 9g
- Net Carbs: 3g

LOW-CARB GREEK YOGURT PARFAIT

SERVINGS: 1 SERVING   🕐 5 MINUTES

Ingredients

- 1 cup plain Greek yogurt (full-fat)
- 1/4 cup chopped nuts (almonds, walnuts)
- 1 tbsp unsweetened coconut flakes
- 1 tsp chia seeds
- 1 tbsp low-carb sweetener (like erythritol)
- 1/4 cup fresh strawberries, sliced

Instruction

1. Layer Greek yogurt in a glass or bowl.
2. Top with nuts, coconut flakes, chia seeds, and sliced strawberries.
3. Drizzle with sweetener and serve.

Nutritional value:

- Calories: 250 kcal
- Protein: 15g
- Carbs: 10g (Net Carbs: 5g)
- Fat: 18g
- Fiber: 5g

Breakfast

CHICKEN AVOCADO SALAD

SERVINGS: 4 SERVING) 🕒 15 MINUTES

Ingredients

- 2 cups cooked chicken breast, shredded or diced
- 2 ripe avocados, diced
- 1 cup cherry tomatoes, halved
- 1 small red onion, finely sliced
- 2 cups mixed greens (spinach, arugula, or lettuce)
- 1/4 cup fresh cilantro, chopped
- 1 lime, juiced
- 2 tablespoons olive oil
- Salt and pepper to taste

Instruction

1. Cook the chicken: If not already cooked, season chicken breast with salt and pepper. Grill, bake, or pan-fry until fully cooked. Allow to cool, then shred or dice.
2. In a small bowl, whisk together lime juice, olive oil, salt, and pepper.
3. In a large bowl, mix together chicken, avocado, cherry tomatoes, red onion, mixed greens, and cilantro.
4. Pour the dressing over the salad and gently toss to coat all ingredients evenly.
5. Serve immediately for the freshest taste.

Nutritional value:

- Calories: 320
- Protein: 25g
- Carbohydrates: 12g
- Total Fat: 22g

CAULIFLOWER HASH BROWNS

SERVINGS: 2 🕒 20 MINUTES

Ingredients

- 2 cups grated cauliflower
- 1 large egg
- 1/4 cup shredded cheddar cheese
- 1/4 tsp garlic powder
- 1/4 tsp salt
- 2 tbsp coconut oil for frying
- 1 tsp chopped parsley (optional)

Instruction

1. Mix grated cauliflower, egg, cheese, garlic powder, and salt in a bowl.
2. Form small patties from the mixture.
3. Heat coconut oil in a skillet over medium heat and fry the patties for 3-4 minutes per side until golden.
4. Garnish with chopped parsley before serving.

Nutritional value:

- Calories: 150 kcal
- Protein: 8g
- Carbs: 5g (Net Carbs: 3g)
- Fat: 12g
- Fiber: 2g

Lunch

TUNA LETTUCE WRAPS

SERVINGS: MAKES 2 WRAPS 🕐 10 MINUTES

Ingredients

- 1 can tuna in water, drained
- 1/4 avocado, mashed
- 1 tbsp mayonnaise
- 1 tbsp chopped celery
- Salt and pepper to taste
- 2 large romaine or butter lettuce leaves

Instruction

1. In a bowl, mix together tuna, avocado, mayonnaise, celery, salt, and pepper.
2. Place the tuna mixture onto each lettuce leaf and wrap tightly.

Nutritional value:

- Calories: 180
- Fat: 10g
- Protein: 16g
- Net Carbs: 2g

AVOCADO TOAST WITH POACHED EGG

SERVINGS: 1 SERVING 🕐 10 MINUTES

Ingredients

- 1 slice whole grain bread
- 1 ripe avocado
- 1 egg
- 1 tsp lemon juice
- Salt & pepper to taste
- A pinch of red chili flakes
- Fresh herbs (like parsley or cilantro) for garnish

Instruction

1. Toast the whole grain bread until golden brown.
2. While the bread is toasting, bring a small pot of water to a gentle simmer. Crack the egg into a small bowl.
3. Swirl the water with a spoon and gently drop the egg in. Let it cook for 3-4 minutes for a runny yolk.
4. Mash the avocado in a bowl, adding lemon juice, salt, and pepper.
5. Spread the avocado mixture on the toasted bread.
6. Top with the poached egg, sprinkle red chili flakes and fresh herbs.

Nutritional value:

- Calories: 300
- Protein: 10g
- Carbohydrates: 25g
- Fat: 20g

Lunch

GREEK KETO SALAD BOWL
SERVINGS: MAKES 1 BOWL 🕐 10 MINUTES

Ingredients

- 1 cup chopped cucumber
- 1/4 cup cherry tomatoes, halved
- 1/4 cup feta cheese, crumbled
- 1/4 cup black olives
- 2 tbsp olive oil
- 1 tbsp red wine vinegar
- Salt and pepper to taste
- 1/2 tsp dried oregano

Instruction

1. In a bowl, add cucumber, cherry tomatoes, feta cheese, and olives.
2. In a small bowl, whisk together olive oil, vinegar, salt, pepper, and oregano.
3. Drizzle dressing over the salad and toss to combine.

Nutritional value:

- Calories: 200
- Fat: 18g
- Protein: 5g
- Net Carbs: 3g

OVERNIGHT OATS
SERVINGS: 1 SERVING 🕐 5 MINUTES

Ingredients

- 1/2 cup rolled oats
- 1/2 cup almond milk (or any milk of choice)
- 1/4 cup Greek yogurt
- 1 tbsp chia seeds
- 1 tsp honey or maple syrup
- 1/4 cup fresh berries (blueberries or strawberries)
- 1 tbsp chopped nuts (almonds or walnuts)

Instruction

1. In a jar or bowl, combine rolled oats, chia seeds, milk, and Greek yogurt.
2. Add honey or maple syrup and mix well.
3. Seal the jar and refrigerate overnight.
4. In the morning, top with fresh berries and nuts before serving.

Nutritional value:

- Calories: 350
- Protein: 15g
- Carbohydrates: 55g
- Fat: 10g
- Fiber: 10g

Lunch

TURKEY & CHEESE ROLL-UPS

SERVINGS: MAKES 2 ROLL-UPS 🕐 5 MINUTES

Ingredients

- 4 slices deli turkey
- 2 slices Swiss or cheddar cheese
- 1/4 avocado, sliced
- 2 tbsp mayonnaise
- 1 cup mixed greens

Instruction

1. Place two slices of turkey flat on a plate and layer with cheese, avocado, mayonnaise, and mixed greens.
2. Roll up tightly and secure with toothpicks if needed. Repeat for the second roll-up.

Nutritional value:

- Calories: 210
- Fat: 14g
- Protein: 16g
- Net Carbs: 2g

VEGGIE OMELET

SERVINGS: 1 SERVING 🕐 15 MINUTES

Ingredients

- 2 eggs
- 1/4 cup diced bell peppers
- 1/4 cup diced tomatoes
- 1/4 cup baby spinach
- 1 tbsp chopped onion
- 1 tbsp grated cheese (optional)
- 1 tsp olive oil
- Salt & pepper to taste

Instruction

1. Beat eggs in a bowl and season with salt and pepper.
2. Heat olive oil in a non-stick pan over medium heat.
3. Sauté onion, bell peppers, and tomatoes for 2-3 minutes.
4. Add spinach and cook for another minute.
5. Pour the beaten eggs over the vegetables and cook for 3-4 minutes.
6. Sprinkle cheese if using and fold the omelet in half. Cook until eggs are set.

Nutritional value:

- Calories: 250
- Protein: 15g
- Carbohydrates: 10g
- Fat: 18g
- Fiber: 3g

Appetizer

CAULIFLOWER FRIED RICE MEAL PREP BOWLS

SERVINGS: MAKES 4 BOWLS | 15 MINUTES

Ingredients

- 2 cups cauliflower rice
- 1 tbsp olive oil
- 1/2 cup diced bell pepper
- 1/2 cup diced zucchini
- 1/4 cup chopped green onions
- 2 eggs, beaten
- 1 tbsp soy sauce or coconut aminos

Instruction

1. Heat olive oil in a skillet over medium heat. Add cauliflower rice and cook until slightly tender.
2. Add bell pepper, zucchini, and green onions, and cook for 5 minutes.
3. Push vegetables to one side, pour in the eggs, and scramble until cooked.
4. Stir in soy sauce and combine. Divide into 4 containers for meal prep.

Nutritional value:

- Calories: 110
- Fat: 7g
- Protein: 5g
- Net Carbs: 4g

BANANA PEANUT BUTTER SMOOTHIE

SERVINGS: 1 SERVING | 5 MINUTES

Ingredients

- 1 ripe banana
- 1 tbsp peanut butter
- 1/2 cup almond milk
- 1/2 cup Greek yogurt
- 1 tsp honey
- A handful of ice cubes

Instruction

1. Add banana, peanut butter, almond milk, Greek yogurt, honey, and ice cubes to a blender.
2. Blend until smooth and creamy.
3. Pour into a glass and serve immediately.

Nutritional value:

- Calories: 300
- Protein: 12g
- Carbohydrates: 40g
- Fat: 12g
- Fiber: 5g

Lunch

KETO COBB SALAD

SERVINGS: MAKES 2 SERVINGS 🕒 15 MINUTES

Ingredients

- 2 cups romaine lettuce, chopped
- 1/2 avocado, diced
- 1 hard-boiled egg, sliced
- 1/4 cup cooked and crumbled bacon
- 1/4 cup cherry tomatoes, halved
- 1/4 cup blue cheese, crumbled
- 2 tbsp olive oil
- 1 tbsp apple cider vinegar
- Salt and pepper to taste

Instruction

1. In a large bowl, layer romaine, avocado, egg, bacon, cherry tomatoes, and blue cheese.
2. Drizzle with olive oil and apple cider vinegar, and season with salt and pepper.

Nutritional value:

- Calories: 350
- Fat: 29g
- Protein: 15g
- Net Carbs: 4g

BERRY AND NUTTY BREAKFAST BOWL

SERVINGS: MAKES 1 SERVINGS 🕒 20 MINUTES

Ingredients

- 1/2 cup quinoa (cooked)
- 1/4 cup mixed berries (blueberries, strawberries)
- 1 tbsp chopped almonds
- 1 tbsp chopped walnuts
- 1 tbsp chia seeds
- 1 tsp maple syrup
- 1/4 cup almond milk

Instruction

1. Cook quinoa according to package instructions and let it cool.
2. In a bowl, combine cooked quinoa, mixed berries, chopped nuts, and chia seeds.
3. Drizzle with maple syrup and add a splash of almond milk.
4. Mix well and serve.

Nutritional value:

- Calories: 350
- Protein: 10g
- Carbohydrates: 60g
- Fat: 12g
- Fiber: 10g

Lunch

KETO EGG SALAD WRAPS

SERVINGS: MAKES 2 WRAPS 🕒 10 MINUTES

Ingredients

- 4 hard-boiled eggs, chopped
- 2 tbsp mayonnaise
- Salt and pepper to taste
- 1 tbsp chopped chives
- 2 large lettuce leaves

Instruction

1. In a bowl, mix eggs, mayonnaise, salt, pepper, and chives.
2. Place egg salad on each lettuce leaf and wrap.

Nutritional value:

- Calories: 180
- Fat: 14g
- Protein: 9g
- Net Carbs: 1g

HEALTHY BREAKFAST BURRITO

SERVINGS: 1 SERVING 🕒 20 MINUTES

Ingredients

- 1 whole wheat tortilla
- 2 scrambled eggs
- 1/4 cup diced bell peppers
- 1/4 cup diced tomatoes
- 1/4 cup black beans (canned, drained)
- 1/4 cup shredded cheese
- 1 tbsp salsa
- 1 tsp olive oil
- Fresh cilantro for garnish

Instruction

1. Heat olive oil in a pan, sauté diced bell peppers and tomatoes for 3-4 minutes.
2. Add black beans and cook for another 2 minutes.
3. Scramble eggs in a separate pan.
4. Warm the tortilla in a pan, then layer the scrambled eggs, vegetable mixture, and shredded cheese in the center.
5. Add salsa and roll the tortilla into a burrito. Garnish with fresh cilantro.

Nutritional value:

- Calories: 400
- Protein: 20g
- Carbohydrates: 45g
- Fat: 15g
- Fiber: 8g

Lunch

KETO CHICKEN CAESAR SALAD
SERVINGS: MAKES 2 SERVINGS 🕐 20 MINUTES

Ingredients

- 2 cups romaine lettuce, chopped
- 1/2 cup cooked chicken breast, sliced
- 2 tbsp Caesar dressing (sugar-free)
- 1/4 cup grated Parmesan cheese
- Salt and pepper to taste

Instruction

1. In a bowl, combine romaine lettuce and chicken breast.
2. Add Caesar dressing and toss to coat.
3. Sprinkle with Parmesan cheese and season with salt and pepper.

Nutritional value:

- Calories: 300
- Fat: 24g
- Protein: 20g
- Net Carbs: 2g

BANANA OATMEAL PANCAKES
SERVINGS: MAKES 2 SERVINGS 🕐 15 MINUTES

Ingredients

- 1 cup rolled oats
- 1 ripe banana
- 1 egg
- 1/4 cup almond milk (or any milk)
- 1/2 tsp baking powder
- 1/4 tsp cinnamon
- 1 tsp vanilla extract
- Cooking spray or 1 tsp coconut oil
- Fresh fruits and honey for topping

Instruction

1. Blend oats, banana, egg, milk, baking powder, cinnamon, and vanilla until smooth.
2. Heat a non-stick pan with coconut oil. Pour 1/4 cup of batter for each pancake.
3. Cook for 2-3 minutes per side until golden brown.
4. Serve with fresh fruits and a drizzle of honey

Nutritional value:

- Calories: 270
- Protein: 8g
- Carbs: 44g
- Fat: 8g
- Fiber: 6g

Lunch

BEEF TACO SALAD BOWL

SERVINGS: MAKES 2 bowls 🕒 15 MINUTES

Ingredients

- 1/2 lb ground beef
- 1 tbsp taco seasoning (no sugar added)
- 2 cups shredded lettuce
- 1/2 avocado, diced
- 1/4 cup shredded cheddar cheese
- 1 tbsp salsa
- 1 tbsp sour cream

Instruction

1. In a skillet, cook ground beef with taco seasoning until fully cooked.
2. Divide lettuce, avocado, cheese, salsa, and sour cream between two bowls.
3. Top with ground beef and serve.

Nutritional value:

- Calories: 400
- Fat: 30g
- Protein: 22g
- Net Carbs: 4g

SPINACH AND MUSHROOM OMELETTE

SERVINGS: MAKES 2 bowls 🕒 15 MINUTES

Ingredients

- 3 large eggs
- 1 cup fresh spinach
- 1/2 cup sliced mushrooms
- 1/4 cup shredded cheese (cheddar or mozzarella)
- Salt and pepper to taste
- 1 tsp olive oil
- Fresh herbs (parsley or chives) for garnish

Instruction

1. Heat olive oil in a non-stick skillet. Sauté mushrooms for 2-3 minutes.
2. Add spinach and cook until wilted. Remove from pan.
3. Beat eggs with salt and pepper, pour into the skillet, and cook until edges firm up.
4. Add mushroom-spinach mix and cheese on one side, fold over, and cook for another 2 minutes.
5. Garnish with herbs and serve.

Nutritional value:

- Calories: 320
- Protein: 20g
- Carbs: 6g
- Fat: 24g
- Fiber: 3g

Lunch **19**

SPINACH & FETA KETO QUICHE

SERVINGS: MAKES 6 SLICES 🕒 30 MINUTES

Ingredients

- 4 large eggs
- 1 cup heavy cream
- Salt and pepper to taste
- 1/2 cup chopped spinach
- 1/4 cup crumbled feta cheese

Instruction

1. Preheat oven to 350°F (175°C).
2. In a bowl, whisk eggs, heavy cream, salt, and pepper.
3. Stir in spinach and feta cheese.
4. Pour mixture into a greased baking dish and bake for 25-30 minutes or until set.

Nutritional value:

- Calories: 400
- Fat: 30g
- Protein: 22g
- Net Carbs: 4g

KETO BREAKFAST CASSEROLE

SERVINGS: MAKES 6 SERVING 🕒 40 MINUTES

Ingredients

- 8 large eggs
- 1 cup cooked bacon, chopped
- 1/2 cup shredded cheddar cheese
- 1/2 cup diced bell peppers
- 1/4 cup heavy cream

Instruction

1. Preheat the oven to 375°F (190°C).
2. In a large bowl, whisk 8 eggs with 1/4 cup heavy cream.
3. Add 1 cup of cooked, chopped bacon, 1/2 cup diced bell peppers, and 1/2 cup shredded cheddar cheese. Mix well.
4. Pour the mixture into a greased baking dish.
5. Bake for 30-35 minutes until the center is set.
6. Cool slightly, cut into portions, and serve.

Nutritional value:

- Calories: 250
- Fat: 20g
- Protein: 15g
- Carbs: 5g
- Fiber: 1g

Lunch

ZUCCHINI NOODLE LASAGNA
SERVINGS: Makes 4 servings 🕐 55 MINUTES

Ingredients

- 2 medium zucchini, thinly sliced lengthwise
- 1 lb ground beef
- 1 cup ricotta cheese
- 1 cup shredded mozzarella cheese
- 1 cup marinara sauce (sugar-free)
- 1 tsp Italian seasoning
- Salt and pepper to taste
- 1 tbsp olive oil

Instruction

1. Preheat oven to 375°F (190°C).
2. In a skillet, heat olive oil and cook ground beef until browned. Season with salt, pepper, and Italian seasoning. Stir in marinara sauce.
3. Layer zucchini slices, beef mixture, ricotta cheese, and mozzarella in a baking dish.
4. Repeat layers, ending with mozzarella on top.
5. Bake for 25-30 minutes until bubbly and golden.

Nutritional value:

- Calories: 380
- Fat: 28g
- Protein: 25g
- Net Carbs: 6g

KETO BULLETPROOF COFFEE
SERVINGS: 1 cups 🕐 5 MINUTES

Ingredients

- 1 cup brewed coffee
- 1 tbsp unsalted butter
- 1 tbsp coconut oil or MCT oil

Instruction

1. Brew 1 cup of your favorite coffee.
2. In a blender, add the hot coffee, 1 tablespoon of unsalted butter, and 1 tablespoon of coconut or MCT oil.
3. Blend on high for 20-30 seconds until creamy and frothy.
4. Pour into a mug and enjoy hot.

Nutritional value:

- Calories: 230
- Fat: 25g
- Protein: 0g
- Carbs: 0g
- Fiber: 0g
- Net Carbs: 0g

Dinner

KETO MEATLOAF WITH ALMOND FLOUR

SERVINGS: Makes 6 slices   🕐 1 Hour

Ingredients

- 1 lb ground beef
- 1/2 cup almond flour
- 1 large egg
- 1/4 cup grated Parmesan cheese
- 1 tbsp Worcestershire sauce
- Salt and pepper to taste
- 1/4 cup sugar-free ketchup

Instruction

1. Preheat oven to 350°F (175°C).
2. In a bowl, mix ground beef, almond flour, egg, Parmesan, Worcestershire sauce, salt, and pepper.
3. Form into a loaf shape and place in a baking dish. Top with sugar-free ketchup.
4. Bake for 45-50 minutes or until cooked through.

Nutritional value:

- Calories: 300
- Fat: 22g
- Protein: 18g
- Net Carbs: 3g

KETO COTTAGE CHEESE AND BERRY BOWL

SERVINGS: 1 Bowl   🕐 5 Minutes

Ingredients

- 1/2 cup full-fat cottage cheese
- 1/4 cup fresh berries (raspberries or strawberries)
- 1 tsp chia seeds

Instruction

1. In a bowl, add 1/2 cup full-fat cottage cheese.
2. Top with 1/4 cup fresh berries of your choice.
3. Sprinkle with 1 teaspoon of chia seeds and enjoy.

Nutritional value:

- Calories: 200
- Fat: 12g
- Protein: 10g
- Carbs: 8g
- Fiber: 2g
- Net Carbs: 6g

Dinner

CHAPTER TWO: WEEKEND TREATS AND ENTERTAINING

KETO WAFFLES
SERVINGS: 2 servings   🕒 15 MINUTES

Ingredients

- 1 cup almond flour
- 2 large eggs
- 1/4 cup unsweetened almond milk1 tsp baking powder
- 1/2 tsp vanilla extract
- 1/4 tsp salt
- Butter or coconut oil for greasing

Instruction

1. Preheat the waffle maker.
2. In a mixing bowl, combine almond flour, baking powder, and salt.
3. In another bowl, whisk together eggs, almond milk, and vanilla extract.
4. Mix the wet ingredients into the dry ingredients until well combined.
5. Grease the waffle maker with butter or coconut oil.
6. Pour the batter into the waffle maker and cook until golden brown.

Nutritional value:

- Calories: 350g
- Fat: 30g
- Protein: 12g
- Carbs: 6g (Net Carbs: 2g)

MINI CAPRESE SKEWERS
SERVINGS: 10 servings   🕒 10 MINUTES

Ingredients

- 20 cherry tomatoes
- 20 small mozzarella balls
- Fresh basil leaves
- 2 tbsp olive oil
- 1 tbsp balsamic glaze
- Salt & pepper to taste

Instruction

1. Thread one cherry tomato, one basil leaf, and one mozzarella ball onto a small skewer.
2. Repeat for the remaining skewers.
3. Drizzle with olive oil, balsamic glaze, salt, and pepper.

Nutritional value:

- Calories: 80
- Protein: 4g
- Fat: 6g
- Carbs: 3g

Breakfast

FRITTATA
SERVINGS: 4 servings 🕐 20 MINUTES

Ingredients

- 6 large eggs
- 1/2 cup heavy cream
- 1 cup spinach, chopped
- 1/2 cup bell pepper, diced
- 1/2 cup cheddar cheese, shredded
- Salt and pepper to taste
- 1 tbsp olive oil

Instruction

1. Preheat the oven to 375°F (190°C).
2. In a bowl, whisk together eggs, heavy cream, salt, and pepper.
3. In an oven-safe skillet, heat olive oil over medium heat. Sauté bell peppers and spinach until softened.
4. Pour the egg mixture into the skillet, then sprinkle cheese on top.
5. Cook on the stove for 2-3 minutes until edges start to set, then transfer to the oven and bake for 15-20 minutes.

Nutritional value:

- Calories: 250
- Fat: 20g
- Protein: 14g
- Carbs: 3g (Net Carbs: 2g)

CLASSIC BRUSCHETTA
SERVINGS: 8 servings 🕐 15 MINUTES

Ingredients

- 1 baguette, sliced
- 4 ripe tomatoes, diced
- 2 cloves garlic, minced
- Fresh basil, chopped
- 1 tbsp olive oil
- Salt & pepper to taste

Instruction

1. Toast the baguette slices until golden.
2. Mix tomatoes, garlic, basil, olive oil, salt, and pepper.
3. Spoon the mixture onto each baguette slice.

Nutritional value:

- Calories: 150
- Protein: 4g
- Fat: 5g
- Carbs: 20g

STUFFED AVOCADO BOATS

SERVINGS: 2 servings   🕒 15 MINUTES

Ingredients

- 2 ripe avocados
- 1 cup cooked chicken, shredded
- 1/4 cup Greek yogurt
- 1/4 cup diced tomatoes
- 1 tbsp lime juice
- Salt and pepper to taste

Instruction

1. Halve the avocados and remove the pits.
2. In a bowl, mix shredded chicken, Greek yogurt, diced tomatoes, lime juice, salt, and pepper.
3. Spoon the mixture into the avocado halves.

Nutritional value:

- Calories: 320g
- Fat: 22g
- Protein: 24g
- Carbs: 8g (Net Carbs: 4g)

LEMON BLUEBERRY SCONES

SERVINGS: 8 scones   🕒 20 MINUTES

Ingredients

- 2 cups all-purpose flour
- 1/4 cup sugar
- 1 tbsp baking powder
- 1/2 tsp salt
- 1/2 cup cold butter, cubed
- 1/2 cup fresh blueberries
- Zest of 1 lemon
- 1/2 cup heavy cream
- 1 large egg
- 1 tsp vanilla extract
- 2 tbsp milk (for brushing)
- Sugar for sprinkling

Instruction

1. Preheat the oven to 400°F (200°C). Line a baking sheet with parchment paper.
2. Mix flour, sugar, baking powder, and salt in a bowl. Cut in cold butter until the mixture is crumbly.
3. Add blueberries and lemon zest. In a separate bowl, whisk cream, egg, and vanilla.
4. Combine wet and dry ingredients. Form dough, pat into a circle, and cut into 8 wedges.
5. Brush with milk and sprinkle sugar on top. Bake for 15 minutes until golden.

Nutritional value:

- Calories: 240
- Protein: 4g
- Fat: 12g
- Carbs: 30g

Appetizer

CHIA SEED PUDDING

SERVINGS: 2 servings   🕐 2 hours

Ingredients

- 1/4 cup chia seeds
- 1 cup unsweetened almond milk
- 1 tbsp sweetener (erythritol or stevia)
- 1/2 tsp vanilla extract
- Fresh berries for topping

Instruction

1. In a bowl, combine chia seeds, almond milk, sweetener, and vanilla extract.
2. Stir well, cover, and refrigerate for at least 2 hours or overnight.
3. Stir again before serving and top with fresh berries.

Nutritional value:

- Calories: 160
- Fat: 9g
- Protein: 5g
- Carbs: 14g (Net Carbs: 12g)

BBQ CHICKEN SLIDERS

SERVINGS: 12 sliders   🕐 25 Minutes

Ingredients

- 12 slider buns
- 2 cups shredded cooked chicken
- 1 cup BBQ sauce
- 1/2 cup shredded mozzarella
- 1/4 cup sliced pickles
- 1/4 red onion, thinly sliced
- 1 tbsp melted butter
- 1 tsp sesame seeds

Instruction

1. Preheat the oven to 350°F (175°C).
2. Mix shredded chicken with BBQ sauce.
3. Slice buns in half, layer with BBQ chicken, mozzarella, pickles, and red onion.
4. Cover with bun tops, brush with melted butter, and sprinkle with sesame seeds.
5. Bake for 15-20 minutes until cheese is melted and buns are toasted.

Nutritional value:

- Calories: 210
- Protein: 10g
- Fat: 6g
- Carbs: 28g

Breakfast

KETO PIZZA
SERVINGS: 4 servings 🕐 25 MINUTES

Ingredients
- 2 cups mozzarella cheese, shredded
- 1/2 cup almond flour
- 2 large eggs
- 1 tsp Italian seasoning
- 1/2 cup sugar-free pizza sauce
- Toppings of choice (pepperoni, bell peppers, olives)

Instruction
1. Preheat the oven to 425°F (220°C).
2. In a bowl, mix shredded mozzarella, almond flour, eggs, and Italian seasoning until combined.
3. Spread the mixture on a parchment-lined baking sheet to form a pizza crust.
4. Bake for 12-15 minutes until golden.
5. Remove from the oven, add pizza sauce and toppings, then return to the oven for an additional 10 minutes.

Nutritional value:
- Calories: 300
- Fat: 20g
- Protein: 18g
- Carbs: 5g (Net Carbs: 3g)

CHEESY GARLIC BREADSTICKS
SERVINGS: 8 breadsticks 🕐 15 MINUTES

Instruction
- 1 can of refrigerated pizza dough
- 2 tbsp butter, melted
- 2 cloves garlic, minced
- 1 cup shredded mozzarella cheese
- 1/4 cup grated Parmesan cheese
- 1 tbsp chopped parsley
- Marinara sauce for dipping

Instruction
1. Preheat oven to 400°F (200°C). Roll out pizza dough and cut into strips.
2. Brush with melted butter and garlic. Sprinkle with mozzarella and Parmesan.
3. Bake for 12-15 minutes. Garnish with parsley. Serve with marinara.

Nutritional value:
- Calories: 180
- Protein: 6g
- Fat: 8g
- Carbs: 20g

Lunch

BURGERS WITH CAULIFLOWER BUNS

SERVINGS: 4 servings 🕒 20 MINUTES

Ingredients

- 1 head cauliflower, riced
- 1 egg
- 1/2 cup shredded mozzarella cheese
- 1 lb ground beef
- Salt and pepper to taste
- Lettuce, tomato, and pickles for toppings

Instruction

1. Preheat the oven to 400°F (200°C).
2. Steam riced cauliflower for 5 minutes and let it cool.
3. Combine cauliflower, egg, and mozzarella cheese. Form into buns and place on a baking sheet.
4. Bake for 15-20 minutes until golden.
5. Cook ground beef patties in a skillet, seasoned with salt and pepper.
6. Assemble burgers with patties and desired toppings in cauliflower buns.

Nutritional value:

- Calories: 350
- Fat: 28g
- Protein: 25g
- Carbs: 4g (Net Carbs: 2g)

STUFFED MUSHROOMS

SERVINGS: 20 mushrooms 🕒 20 MINUTES

Ingredients

- 20 large white mushrooms
- 1/2 cup cream cheese
- 1/4 cup grated Parmesan cheese
- 1/4 cup breadcrumbs
- 2 cloves garlic, minced
- 1 tbsp chopped parsley
- Salt and pepper to taste

Instruction

1. Preheat oven to 375°F (190°C). Remove mushroom stems.
2. Mix cream cheese, Parmesan, breadcrumbs, garlic, and parsley. Season with salt and pepper.
3. Stuff each mushroom cap with mixture.
4. Bake for 20 minutes.

Nutritional value:

- Calories: 50
- Protein: 2g
- Fat: 4g
- Carbs: 3g

Lunch

BUFFALO WINGS

SERVINGS: 4 servings   🕐 40 MINUTES

Ingredients

- 2 lbs chicken wings
- 1/2 cup hot sauce
- 1/4 cup unsalted butter, melted
- 1 tbsp vinegar
- Salt and pepper to taste

Instruction

1. Preheat the oven to 400°F (200°C).
2. Season chicken wings with salt and pepper and arrange them on a baking sheet.
3. Bake for 40-45 minutes until crispy.
4. In a bowl, mix hot sauce, melted butter, and vinegar.
5. Toss baked wings in the sauce and serve hot.

Nutritional value:

- Calories: 400
- Fat: 30g
- Protein: 30g
- Carbs: 0g

CHOCOLATE-DIPPED STRAWBERRIES

SERVINGS: 20 strawberries   🕐 15 MINUTES

Ingredients

- 20 fresh strawberries
- 1 cup dark chocolate chips
- 1 tsp coconut oil
- Sprinkles or chopped nuts (optional)

Instruction

1. Melt chocolate chips and coconut oil in a microwave.
2. Dip strawberries in melted chocolate and place on parchment paper.
3. Decorate with sprinkles or nuts. Chill until set.

Nutritional value:

- Calories: 60
- Protein: 1g
- Fat: 3g
- Carbs: 8g

Appetizer

ZUCCHINI NOODLES WITH PESTO

SERVINGS: 2 servings 🕒 15 MINUTES

Ingredients

- 2 large zucchinis, spiralized
- 1/2 cup basil pesto (store-bought or homemade)
- 1/4 cup cherry tomatoes, halved
- Salt and pepper to taste
- Grated Parmesan cheese for serving

Instruction

1. Heat a skillet over medium heat. Add zucchini noodles and sauté for 3-4 minutes until tender.
2. Stir in pesto and cherry tomatoes, cooking for another 2 minutes.
3. Season with salt and pepper, and serve topped with grated Parmesan.

Nutritional value:

- Calories: 180
- Fat: 14g
- Protein: 6g
- Carbs: 8g (Net Carbs: 5g)

CINNAMON SUGAR CHURROS

SERVINGS: 12 churros 🕒 15 MINUTES

Ingredients

- 1 tbsp sugar
- 1 cup all-purpose flour
- 2 large eggs
- 1/2 cup sugar
- 1 tsp cinnamon
- Vegetable oil for frying

Instruction

1. In a saucepan, bring water, butter, and 1 tbsp of sugar to a boil. Remove from heat and stir in flour until a dough forms.
2. Let it cool slightly, then beat in eggs one at a time until smooth.
3. Heat oil in a deep pan to 350°F (175°C).
4. Transfer dough to a piping bag with a star tip and pipe 4-inch strips into the hot oil. Fry until golden brown, about 2-3 minutes per side.
5. Mix 1/2 cup sugar and cinnamon. Roll warm churros in the mixture

Nutritional value:

- Calories: 160
- Protein: 3g
- Fat: 8g
- Carbs: 20g

Dinner

BACON-WRAPPED JALAPEÑOS

SERVINGS: 6 servings 🕐 20 MINUTES

Ingredients
- 12 jalapeños, halved and seeded
- 8 oz cream cheese, softened
- 12 slices bacon
- 1/2 cup shredded cheddar cheese (optional)

Instruction
1. Preheat the oven to 375°F (190°C).
2. Fill jalapeño halves with cream cheese and sprinkle with cheddar cheese if using.
3. Wrap each stuffed jalapeño with a slice of bacon and secure with a toothpick.
4. Bake for 20-25 minutes until bacon is crispy.

Nutritional value:
- Calories: 250
- Fat: 20g
- Protein: 12g
- Carbs: 4g (Net Carbs: 2g)

PROSCIUTTO & MELON BITES

SERVINGS: 16 bites 🕐 10 MINUTES

Ingredients
- 1/2 cantaloupe, cut into cubes
- 8 slices of prosciutto, halved
- 16 fresh basil leaves
- 1 tbsp balsamic glaze
- 16 toothpicks

Instruction
1. Wrap each melon cube with half a slice of prosciutto and secure with a toothpick.
2. Place a basil leaf on top and drizzle with balsamic glaze.
3. Serve immediately for a refreshing appetizer.

Nutritional value:
- Calories: 35
- Protein: 2g
- Fat: 2g
- Carbs: 3g

Small bite

CAULIFLOWER BITES

SERVINGS: 4 servings 30 MINUTES

Ingredients

- 1 head cauliflower, cut into florets
- 1/4 cup olive oil
- 1 tsp garlic powder
- 1 tsp paprika
- Salt and pepper to taste

Instruction

1. Preheat the oven to 425°F (220°C).
2. Toss cauliflower florets with olive oil, garlic powder, paprika, salt, and pepper.
3. Spread on a baking sheet and roast for 20-25 minutes until golden and tender.

Nutritional value:

- Calories: 120
- Fat: 9g
- Protein: 4g
- Carbs: 8g (Net Carbs: 5g)

CRISPY PARMESAN ZUCCHINI FRIES

SERVINGS: 4 servings 10 MINUTES

Ingredients

- 2 large zucchinis, cut into sticks
- 1 cup panko breadcrumbs
- 1/2 cup grated Parmesan cheese
- 1 tsp garlic powder
- 1 tsp dried Italian herbs
- 2 large eggs, beaten
- Salt and pepper to taste
- Marinara sauce for dipping

Instruction

1. Preheat oven to 425°F (220°C). Line a baking sheet with parchment paper.
2. Mix panko, Parmesan, garlic powder, and herbs in a bowl. Dip zucchini sticks in egg, then coat with breadcrumb mixture.
3. Place on the baking sheet and bake for 20 minutes, turning halfway.
4. Serve with marinara sauce.

Nutritional value:

- Calories: 150
- Protein: 7g
- Fat: 5g
- Carbs: 18g

Small bite

SPINACH AND CHEESE STUFFED MUSHROOMS

SERVINGS: 4 servings   15 MINUTES

Ingredients

- 12 large mushrooms, stems removed
- 1 cup spinach, chopped
- 1/2 cup cream cheese, softened
- 1/4 cup Parmesan cheese, grated
- Salt and pepper to taste

Instruction

1. Preheat the oven to 375°F (190°C).
2. In a bowl, mix spinach, cream cheese, Parmesan, salt, and pepper.
3. Stuff each mushroom cap with the mixture.
4. Arrange on a baking sheet and bake for 20 minutes until mushrooms are tender.

Nutritional value:

- Calories: 350
- Fat: 28g
- Protein: 20g
- Carbs: 5g (Net Carbs: 3g)

PESTO PINWHEELS

SERVINGS: 16 pinwheels   17 MINUTES

Ingredients

- 1 sheet puff pastry, thawed
- 1/4 cup basil pesto
- 1/4 cup shredded mozzarella cheese
- 1 tbsp grated Parmesan
- 1 egg, beaten

Instruction

1. Preheat oven to 400°F (200°C). Roll out puff pastry and spread with pesto.
2. Sprinkle with mozzarella and Parmesan. Roll up tightly and slice into 16 pieces.
3. Brush with beaten egg and bake for 12 minutes or until golden brown.

Nutritional value:

- Calories: 80
- Protein: 2g
- Fat: 5g
- Carbs: 8g

Appetizer

CHAPTER THREE: SNACKS AND ON-THE-GO OPTIONS

CHEESE CRISPS

SERVINGS: 12 cheese crisps. 🕐 10 MINUTES

Ingredients

- 1 cup shredded cheddar cheese
- 1/2 tsp garlic powder
- 1/4 tsp chili powder (optional)
- Parchment paper

Instruction

1. Preheat your oven to 400°F (200°C).
2. Line a baking sheet with parchment paper.
3. In a bowl, mix the shredded cheddar cheese, garlic powder, and chili powder.
4. Spoon small mounds of the cheese mixture onto the parchment paper, spacing them about 2 inches apart.
5. Bake for 5-7 minutes, or until the edges are golden.
6. Allow to cool before enjoying.

Nutritional value:

- Calories: 170
- Protein: 10g
- Fat: 14g
- Carbohydrates: 1g
- Fiber: 0g

NO-BAKE ENERGY BITES

SERVINGS: 20 bites 🕐 15 MINUTES

Ingredients

- 1/3 cup honey or maple syrup
- 1/2 cup ground flaxseed
- 1/4 cup chocolate chips (optional)
- 1/4 cup chia seeds

Instruction

1. In a large bowl, mix all ingredients until well combined.
2. Roll the mixture into small balls (about 1 inch in diameter).
3. Refrigerate for 1 hour before serving.

Nutritional value:

- Calories: 100
- Protein: 3g
- Carbohydrates: 12g
- Fat: 5g
- Fiber: 2g

Appetizer

AVOCADO DEVILED EGGS

SERVINGS: Makes 8 deviled egg   🕐 10 MINUTES

Ingredients

- 4 large eggs
- 1 ripe avocado
- 1 tsp lime juice
- Salt and pepper, to taste
- Paprika, for garnish

Instruction

1. Hard boil the eggs by placing them in a pot of water, bringing it to a boil, then covering and letting sit for 10-12 minutes.
2. Remove the eggs, cool them in ice water, then peel.
3. Cut the eggs in half and remove the yolks.
4. In a bowl, mash the yolks with the avocado and lime juice. Season with salt and pepper.
5. Spoon or pipe the avocado mixture back into the egg white halves.
6. Sprinkle paprika on top for garnish.

Nutritional value:

- Calories: 80
- Protein: 4g
- Fat: 7g
- Carbohydrates: 2g
- Fiber: 1g

HUMMUS & VEGGIE WRAP

SERVINGS: 1 wrap   🕐 15 MINUTES

Ingredients

- 1 whole wheat tortilla
- 1/4 cup hummus
- 1/2 cup sliced cucumber
- 1/2 cup shredded carrots
- 1/4 cup bell peppers, sliced
- 1 handful of spinach leaves

Instruction

1. Spread hummus evenly over the tortilla.
2. Layer cucumber, carrots, bell peppers, and spinach on top.
3. Roll the tortilla tightly and slice in half.

Nutritional value:

- Calories: 250
- Protein : 7g
- Carbohydrates: 32g
- Fat: 10g
- Fiber: 7g

Appetizer

ZUCCHINI CHIPS

SERVINGS: Makes 4 servings   🕐 15 MINUTES

Ingredients

- 2 medium zucchinis
- 2 tbsp olive oil
- 1 tsp sea salt
- 1/2 tsp black pepper
- 1/2 tsp garlic powder

Instruction

1. Preheat your oven to 225°F (110°C).
2. Thinly slice zucchinis using a mandoline or knife.
3. In a bowl, mix olive oil, sea salt, black pepper, and garlic powder.
4. Toss zucchini slices in the oil mixture until uniformly coated.
5. Place the zucchini slices in a single layer on a baking sheet.
6. Bake for 2-3 hours, flipping halfway, until they are crisp.

Nutritional value:

- Calories: 75
- Protein: 2g
- Fat: 5g
- Carbohydrates: 7g
- Fiber: 2g

CRISPY CHICKPEAS

SERVINGS: 2 servings   🕐 30 MINUTES

Ingredients

- 1 can chickpeas, drained and rinsed
- 1 tbsp olive oil
- 1/2 tsp paprika
- 1/2 tsp garlic powder
- 1/2 tsp sea salt

Instruction

1. Preheat oven to 400°F (200°C).
2. Pat chickpeas dry with a paper towel.
3. Toss with olive oil and seasonings.
4. Spread chickpeas on a baking sheet and bake for 20-30 minutes, shaking halfway.

Nutritional value:

- Calories: 120
- Protein: 5g
- Carbohydrates: 17g
- Fat: 5g
- Fiber: 5g

Appetizer

NUT BUTTER ENERGY BALLS

SERVINGS: 18 energy balls   🕒   10 MINUTES

Ingredients

- 1 cup rolled oats
- 1/2 cup nut butter (almond, peanut, or cashew)
- 1/3 cup honey or maple syrup
- 1/4 cup flaxseed meal
- 1/4 cup chocolate chips (optional)
- 1/4 cup shredded coconut (optional)
- 1 tsp vanilla extract

Instruction

1. In a large bowl, mix together the rolled oats, nut butter, honey, flaxseed meal, and vanilla extract.
2. Stir in the chocolate chips and shredded coconut if using.
3. Once combined, refrigerate for about 30 minutes to firm up.
4. Once chilled, roll the mixture into small balls (about 1 inch in diameter).
5. Store in an airtight container in the refrigerator for up to a week.

Nutritional value:

- Calories: 150
- Protein: 4g
- Fat: 12g
- Carbohydrates: 7g
- Fiber: 4g

STUFFED DATES WITH GOAT CHEESE AND ALMONDS

SERVINGS: 10 stuffed dates   🕒   15 MINUTES

Ingredients

- 10 Medjool dates, pitted
- 10 whole almonds
- 1 tsp honey (optional)

Instruction

1. Slice yes
2. Fill each date with a small amount of goat cheese and press an almond into the center.
3. Drizzle with honey if desired.

Nutritional value:

- Calories:
- Protein: 2g
- Carbohydrates: 10g
- Fat: 3g
- Fiber: 1g

Small bite

MINI QUICHES

SERVINGS: Makes 12 mini quiches   🕒 20 MINUTES

Ingredients

- 6 large eggs
- 1 cup milk
- 1 cup chopped vegetables (spinach, bell peppers, onions, etc.)
- 1 cup shredded cheese (cheddar, feta, or mozzarella)
- Salt and pepper, to taste
- Optional: cooked bacon or sausage bits

Instruction

1. Preheat your oven to 375°F (190°C).
2. In a mixing bowl, whisk together eggs, milk, salt, and pepper.
3. Grease a muffin tin and distribute the chopped vegetables and meat (if using) evenly among the muffin cups.
4. Pour the egg mixture over the vegetables, filling each cup about 2/3 full.
5. Top with shredded cheese.
6. Bake for 20-25 minutes, until the quiches are puffed and set.
7. Allow to cool slightly before removing from the muffin tin.

Nutritional value:

- Calories: 150
- Protein: 10g
- Carbohydrates: 2g
- Sugars: 1g
- Fat: 11g

HARD-BOILED EGGS WITH AVOCADO

SERVINGS: 1 serving   🕒 10 MINUTES

Ingredients

- 2 large eggs
- 1/2 avocado
- 1/4 tsp sea salt
- 1/4 tsp black pepper
- 1/2 tsp lemon juice

Instruction

1. Boil eggs for 10 minutes, then cool and peel.
2. Slice the eggs in half and scoop out some yolk.
3. Mash avocado with salt, pepper, and lemon juice.
4. Fill the egg whites with the avocado mixture.

Nutritional value:

- Calories: 220
- Protein: 12g
- Carbohydrates: 5g
- Fat: 17g
- Fiber: 5g

Small bite

TRAIL MIX ENERGY BARS

SERVINGS: 12 bars 🕒 25 MINUTES

Ingredients

- 2 cups rolled oats
- 1 cup mixed nuts (almonds, walnuts, cashews)
- 1/2 cup dried fruit (cranberries, apricots, or raisins)
- 1/2 cup nut butter
- 1/3 cup honey or maple syrup
- 1 tsp vanilla extract
- Pinch of salt

Instruction

1. Preheat your oven to 350°F (175°C) and line an 8x8 inch baking dish with parchment paper.
2. In a large bowl, mix the oats, nuts, and dried fruit.
3. In a small saucepan, blend nut butter, honey, vanilla extract, and salt over medium heat until smooth.
4. Pour the nut butter mixture over the dry ingredients, stirring until well combined.
5. Press the mixture firmly into the prepared baking dish.
6. Bake for 20 minutes or until slightly golden.
7. Allow to cool completely before cutting into bars.

Nutritional value:

- Calories: 200
- Protein: 6g
- Carbohydrates: 27g
- Fat: 9g

CUCUMBER AND SMOKED SALMON BITES

SERVINGS: 5 bites. 🕒 30 MINUTES

Ingredients

- 1 large cucumber, sliced into rounds
- 3 oz smoked salmon, cut into pieces
- 2 tbsp cream cheese
- 1 tbsp chopped fresh dill
- 1 tsp lemon zest

Instruction

1. Spread a small amount of cream cheese on each cucumber slice.
2. Top with a piece of smoked salmon.
3. Garnish with dill and lemon zest.

Nutritional value:

- Calories: 120
- Protein: 8g
- Carbohydrates: 5g
- Fat: 8g
- Fiber: 1g

Appetizer

SWEET POTATO HUMMUS
SERVINGS: Makes about 2 cups 🕒 10 MINUTES

Ingredients
- 1 medium sweet potato (about 1 cup cooked and mashed)
- 1 can (15 oz) chickpeas, drained and rinsed
- 2 tbsp tahini
- 2 tbsp olive oil
- 1 clove garlic
- Juice of 1 lemon
- Salt and pepper, to taste
- Optional: paprika or cumin for flavor

Instruction
1. Peel and chop the sweet potato, then boil until tender (about 15 minutes). Drain and let cool.
2. In a food processor, combine the sweet potato, chickpeas, tahini, olive oil, garlic, lemon juice, salt, and pepper.
3. Blend until smooth, adding a little water if necessary to reach desired consistency.
4. Taste and adjust seasoning if needed. Add paprika or cumin for an extra flavor boost.
5. Transfer to a serving bowl and refrigerate until ready to serve.

Nutritional value:
- Calories: 100
- Protein: 3g
- Carbohydrates: 16g
- Fat: 3g

TOMATO & MOZZARELLA SALAD
SERVINGS: 2 serving 🕒 5 MINUTES

Ingredients
- 1 cup cherry tomatoes, halved
- 1/2 cup mini mozzarella balls
- 1 tbsp fresh basil, chopped
- 1 tbsp balsamic vinegar
- 1 tbsp olive oil
- 1/4 tsp salt
- 1/4 tsp black pepper

Instruction
1. In a bowl, combine cherry tomatoes, mozzarella balls, and chopped basil.
2. Drizzle with balsamic vinegar and olive oil.
3. Season with salt and pepper. Toss gently to mix.

Nutritional value:
- Calories: 180
- Protein : 7g
- Carbohydrates: 8g
- Fat: 14g
- Fiber: 2g

Appetizer

KETO CHOCOLATE CHIP COOKIES
SERVINGS: 12 cookies. 🕐 15 MINUTES

Ingredients
- 1 cup almond flour
- 1/4 cup coconut flour
- 1/2 teaspoon baking soda
- 1/4 teaspoon salt
- 1/2 cup unsalted butter, softened
- 1/3 cup erythritol or preferred low-carb sweetener
- 1 large egg
- 1 teaspoon vanilla extract
- 1/2 cup sugar-free chocolate chips

Instruction
1. Preheat your oven to 350°F (175°C).
2. In a bowl, mix together almond flour, coconut flour, baking soda, and salt.
3. In another bowl, cream together the softened butter and erythritol until fluffy.
4. Add the egg and vanilla extract to the butter mixture, mixing well.
5. Fold in the sugar-free chocolate chips.
6. Drop tablespoon-sized dollops of dough onto a baking sheet lined with parchment paper.
7. Bake for 10-12 minutes or until the edges are golden.
8. Allow cooling on a wire rack before serving.

Nutritional value:
- Calories: 100
- Fat: 9g
- Carbohydrates: 3g

BAKED SWEET POTATO CHIPS
SERVINGS: 4 serving 🕐 30 MINUTES

Ingredients
- 2 large sweet potatoes
- 1 tbsp olive oil
- 1/2 tsp sea salt
- 1/4 tsp paprika
- 1/4 tsp garlic powder

Instruction
1. Preheat the oven to 375°F (190°C).
2. Thinly slice the sweet potatoes using a mandolin or a sharp knife.
3. Toss slices in olive oil and season with salt, paprika, and garlic powder.
4. Spread them evenly on a baking sheet lined with parchment paper.
5. Bake for 20-25 minutes, flipping halfway through, until crisp.

Nutritional value:
- Calories: 110
- Protein: 2g
- Fat: 3.5g
- Carbs: 18g
- Fiber: 3g

Appetizer

KETO STRAWBERRY CHEESECAKE BITES

SERVINGS: 8 bites.   30 MINUTES

Ingredients

- 4 oz cream cheese, softened
- 1/4 cup erythritol or preferred low-carb sweetener
- 1/2 teaspoon vanilla extract
- 1/3 cup fresh strawberries, pureed
- 2 tablespoons almond flour
- 1/4 cup unsweetened shredded coconut (optional)

Instruction

1. In a mixing bowl, beat the softened cream cheese and erythritol together until smooth.
2. Mix in the vanilla extract and pureed strawberries.
3. Stir in the almond flour until well combined.
4. Refrigerate the mixture for about 20 minutes to firm up.
5. Once firm, scoop the mixture into small balls and roll in shredded coconut if desired.
6. Place the bites back in the refrigerator to chill before serving.

Nutritional value:

- Calories: 70
- Fat: 6g
- Carbohydrates: 3g

AVOCADO TOAST

SERVINGS: 1 serving.   10 MINUTES

Ingredients

- 2 slices whole grain bread
- 1 ripe avocado
- 1 tsp lemon juice
- Salt and pepper to taste
- Optional toppings: cherry tomatoes, red pepper flakes, poached egg

Instruction

1. Toast the bread slices until golden.
2. Mash the avocado in a bowl and mix with lemon juice, salt, and pepper.
3. Spread the avocado mixture on the toasted bread.
4. Add optional toppings like cherry tomatoes or a poached egg.

Nutritional value:

- Calories: 250
- Protein: 6g
- Fat: 16g
- Carbs: 26g
- Fiber: 8g

Appetizer

CHAPTER FOUR: COCKTAIL AND BEVERAGE RECIPES

KETO MARGARITA
SERVINGS: 1 glass　　 5 MINUTES

Ingredients

- 2 oz tequila
- 1 oz freshly squeezed lime juice
- 1 oz sugar-free simple syrup (made from erythritol or monk fruit sweetener)
- Ice
- Salt (for rim)

Instruction

1. Rim a glass with salt by rubbing a lime wedge around the rim and dipping it in salt.
2. In a cocktail shaker, add tequila, lime juice, sugar-free simple syrup, and ice.
3. Shake well and strain into the glass over ice.

Nutritional value:

- Approximately 100 calories
- 0g carbs
- 0g fat
- 0g protein

PIÑA COLADA
SERVINGS: 1 glass　　 10 MINUTES

Ingredients

- 2 oz white rum
- 1 oz coconut cream
- 1 oz heavy cream
- 6 oz fresh pineapple juice
- 1 cup crushed ice
- Pineapple slice and cherry for garnish

Instruction

- Blend rum, coconut cream, heavy cream, pineapple juice, and crushed ice until smooth.
- Pour into a chilled glass.
- Garnish with a pineapple slice and a cherry.

Nutritional value:

- Calories: 300 kcal
- Carbs: 35g
- Sugars: 30g
- Protein: 1g
- Fat: 7g

Lunch

KETO MOJITO

SERVINGS: 1 glass 🕐 7 MINUTES

Ingredients

- 2 oz white rum
- 1 oz lime juice
- 1 tbsp sugar-free sweetener
- Fresh mint leaves
- Club soda
- Ice

Instruction

1. Muddle mint leaves and sweetener in a glass.
2. Add lime juice, rum, and ice.
3. Top with club soda and stir.

Nutritional value:

- Approximately 100 calories
- 1g carbs
- 0g fat
- 0g protein

STRAWBERRY DAIQUIRI

SERVINGS: 1 glass 🕐 5 MINUTES

Ingredients

- 2 oz white rum
- 1 oz simple syrup
- 1 oz lime juice
- 4-5 fresh strawberries
- 1 cup ice

Instruction

1. Blend rum, simple syrup, lime juice, strawberries, and ice until smooth.
2. Pour into a glass.
3. Garnish with a strawberry.

Nutritional value:

- Calories: 180 kcal
- Carbs: 22g
- Sugars: 18g
- Protein: 0.5g
- Fat: 0g

Dinner

KETO OLD FASHIONED
SERVINGS: 1 glass   🕒   5 MINUTES

Ingredients

- 2 oz bourbon or rye whiskey
- 2-3 drops of liquid stevia
- Few dashes of Angostura bitters
- Orange peel for garnish

Instruction

1. Combine whiskey, stevia, and bitters in a glass with ice.
2. Stir until well-chilled.
3. Garnish with an orange peel twist.

Nutritional value:

- Approximately 140 calories
- 0g carbs
- 0g fat
- 0g protein

COSMOPOLITAN
SERVINGS: 1 glass   🕒   5 MINUTES

Ingredients

- 1 1/2 oz vodka
- 1 oz cranberry juice
- 1/2 oz Cointreau
- 1/2 oz lime juice
- Lime twist for garnish

Instruction

1. Shake vodka, cranberry juice, Cointreau, and lime juice with ice.
2. Strain into a chilled martini glass.
3. Garnish with a lime twist.

Nutritional value:

- Calories: 210 kcal
- Carbs: 12g
- Sugars: 10g
- Protein: 0g
- Fat: 0g

Lunch

KETO FLAVORED SPARKLING WATER

SERVINGS: 1 glass   🕒 5 MINUTES

Ingredients

- 8 oz sparkling water
- 1-2 slices of cucumber, lemon, or lime
- Fresh mint leaves

Instruction

1. Pour sparkling water into a glass with ice.
2. Add your choice of fresh fruit slices and mint for a refreshing taste.

Nutritional value:

- Approximately 0 calories
- 0g carbs
- 0g fat
- 0g protein

WHISKEY SOUR

SERVINGS: 1 glass   🕒 5 MINUTES

Ingredients

- 2 oz bourbon whiskey
- 3/4 oz fresh lemon juice
- 1/2 oz simple syrup
- Ice
- Maraschino cherry for garnish

Instruction

1. Shake bourbon, lemon juice, and simple syrup with ice.
2. Strain into a glass filled with ice.
3. Garnish with a cherry.

Nutritional value:

- Calories: 170 kcal
- Carbs: 10g
- Sugars: 8g
- Protein: 0g
- Fat: 0g

Lunch

KETO ICED TEA

SERVINGS: 1 glass • 5 MINUTES

Ingredients

- 1 bag of black or green tea
- 8 oz hot water
- Ice
- Lemon wedge
- Stevia or monk fruit sweetener (optional)

Instruction

1. Steep the tea bag in hot water for 3-5 minutes.
2. Pour over ice and add sweetener if desired.
3. Garnish with a lemon wedge.

Nutritional value:

- Approximately 0 calories
- 0g carbs
- 0g fat
- 0g protein

MAI TAI

SERVINGS: 1 glass • 7 MINUTES

Ingredients

- 1 oz white rum
- 1 oz dark rum
- 1/2 oz orange curaçao
- 1/2 oz orgeat syrup
- 1 oz fresh lime juice
- Mint sprig for garnish

Instruction

1. Shake all ingredients with ice.
2. Strain into a glass filled with ice.
3. Garnish with a mint sprig.

Nutritional value:

- Calories: 230 kcal
- Carbs: 14g
- Sugars: 12g
- Protein: 0g
- Fat: 0g

Dinner

KETO COLD BREW COFFEE

SERVINGS: 1 glass 15 minutes

Ingredients

- 8 oz cold brew coffee
- 2-3 tbsp heavy cream
- Liquid stevia (optional)

Instruction

1. Pour cold brew coffee into a glass with ice.
2. Add heavy cream and sweetener as desired.

Nutritional value:

- Approximately 50 calories
- 0g carbs
- 5g fat
- 0g protein

ESPRESSO MARTINI

SERVINGS: 1 glass 7 minutes

Ingredients

- 2 oz vodka
- 1 oz coffee liqueur
- 1 oz freshly brewed espresso
- 1/2 oz simple syrup
- Coffee beans for garnish

Instruction

1. Shake vodka, coffee liqueur, espresso, and simple syrup with ice.
2. Strain into a chilled martini glass.
3. Garnish with coffee beans.

Nutritional value:

- Calories: 190 kcal
- Carbs: 15g
- Sugars: 12g
- Protein: 0g
- Fat: 0g

Breakfast

KETO LEMONADE
SERVINGS: 1 glass 🕒 7 MINUTES

Ingredients
- 1 cup water
- Juice of 1 lemon
- 1-2 tbsp erythritol or monk fruit sweetener

Instruction
1. Combine water, lemon juice, and sweetener in a glass. Stir well.
2. Add ice and garnish with lemon slices.

Nutritional value:
- Approximately 5 calories
- 0g carbs
- 0g fat
- 0g protein

TEQUILA SUNRISE
SERVINGS: 1 glass 🕒 7 MINUTES

Ingredients
- 2 oz tequila
- 4 oz orange juice
- 1/2 oz grenadine
- Ice
- Orange slice and cherry for garnish

Instruction
1. Fill a glass with ice and pour tequila and orange juice over it.
2. Slowly pour grenadine down the side of the glass; it will sink and then slowly rise.
3. Garnish with an orange slice and a cherry.

Nutritional value:
- Calories: 230 kcal
- Carbs: 24g
- Sugars: 20g
- Protein: 1g
- Fat: 0g

Lunch

KETO MATCHA LATTE
SERVINGS: 1 glass   🕒 5 MINUTES

Ingredients
- 1 tsp matcha powder
- 1/4 cup hot water
- 3/4 cup unsweetened almond milk
- Stevia (optional)

Instruction
1. Whisk matcha powder with hot water until smooth.
2. Heat almond milk and pour over matcha. Add sweetener if desired.

Nutritional value:
- Approximately 40 calories
- 1g carbs
- 3g fat
- 1g protein

LONG ISLAND ICED TEA
SERVINGS: 1 glass   🕒 5 MINUTES

Ingredients
- 1/2 oz vodka
- 1/2 oz gin
- 1/2 oz white rum
- 1/2 oz tequila
- 1/2 oz triple sec
- 1 oz lemon juice
- 1 oz simple syrup
- Splash of cola
- Lemon wedge for garnish

Instruction
1. Fill a glass with ice.
2. Add vodka, gin, rum, tequila, triple sec, lemon juice, and simple syrup.
3. Stir gently, top with a splash of cola.
4. Garnish with a lemon wedge.

Nutritional value:
- Calories: 275 kcal
- Carbs: 28g
- Sugars: 26g
- Protein: 0g
- Fat: 0g

Breakfast

KETO HOT CHOCOLATE
SERVINGS: 1 glass   🕒 5 MINUTES

Ingredients
- 1 cup unsweetened almond milk
- 1 tbsp cocoa powder
- 1 tbsp heavy cream
- Stevia to taste

Instruction
1. Heat almond milk and cocoa powder in a saucepan.
2. Stir in heavy cream and sweetener until smooth.

Nutritional value:
- Approximately 80 calories
- 2g carbs
- 7g fat
- 1g protein

KETO BLOODY MARY
SERVINGS: 1 glass   🕒 5 MINUTES

Ingredients
- 1 1/2 oz vodka
- 3 oz sugar-free tomato juice
- 1/2 oz lemon juice
- 2 dashes hot sauce
- 2 dashes Worcestershire sauce (check for sugar-free)
- Pinch of salt and pepper
- Celery stick for garnish

Instruction
1. Stir vodka, tomato juice, lemon juice, hot sauce, Worcestershire, salt, and pepper with ice.
2. Strain into a glass over ice.
3. Garnish with a celery stick.

Nutritional value:
- Calories: 100 kcal
- Carbs: 3g
- Sugars: 1g
- Protein: 1g
- Fat: 0g

Breakfast

KETO CHAI TEA LATTE

SERVINGS: 1 glass   🕒 7 MINUTES

Ingredients

- 1 chai tea bag
- 1/2 cup hot water
- 1/2 cup unsweetened almond milk
- 1 tbsp heavy cream
- Stevia (optional)

Instruction

1. Brew the tea bag in hot water, then add almond milk and heavy cream.
2. Stir in sweetener if desired.

Nutritional value:

- Approximately 70 calories
- 1g carbs
- 7g fat
- 1g protein

KETO COLLINS

SERVINGS: 1 glass   🕒 5 MINUTES

Ingredients

- 2 oz gin
- 1 oz lemon juice
- 1/2 oz sugar-free simple syrup
- 4 oz sparkling water
- Ice
- Lemon slice for garnish

Instruction

1. Shake gin, lemon juice, and sugar-free simple syrup with ice.
2. Strain into a glass with ice.
3. Top with sparkling water and stir gently.
4. Garnish with a lemon slice.

Nutritional value:

- Calories: 90 kcal
- Carbs: 2g
- Sugars: 0g
- Protein: 0g
- Fat: 0g

Breakfast

KETO VANILLA ALMOND MILK LATTE

SERVINGS: 1 glass   🕒 3 MINUTES

Ingredients

- 1 cup unsweetened almond milk
- 1 tsp vanilla extract
- Liquid stevia to taste

Instruction

1. Heat almond milk and vanilla in a saucepan until warmed.
2. Add stevia, stir, and pour into a glass or mug.

Nutritional value:

- Approximately 30 calories
- 1g carbs
- 2g fat
- 1g protein

KETO LEMONADE VODKA SPRITZER

SERVINGS: 1 glass   🕒 3 MINUTES

Ingredients

- 2 oz vodka
- 1 oz fresh lemon juice
- 1 oz sugar-free lemonade
- 4 oz sparkling water
- Ice
- Lemon slice for garnish

Instruction

1. Fill a glass with ice.
2. Add vodka, lemon juice, and sugar-free lemonade.
3. Top with sparkling water, stir gently.
4. Garnish with a lemon slice.

Nutritional value:

- Calories: 100 kcal
- Carbs: 1g
- Sugars: 0g
- Protein: 0g
- Fat: 0g

Breakfast

CHAPTER FIVE: DESSERTS AND SWEET TREATS
QUICK DESSERTS

CHOCOLATE AVOCADO MOUSSE
SERVINGS: 2   🕒 10 MINUTES

Ingredients
- 1 ripe avocado
- 2 tbsp unsweetened cocoa powder
- 2 tbsp almond milk (or any milk alternative)
- 2 tbsp keto-friendly sweetener (like erythritol or stevia)
- 1 tsp vanilla extract
- Pinch of salt
- Fresh berries and whipped cream for garnish (optional)

Instruction
1. Cut the avocado, remove the pit, and scoop out the flesh into a blender.
2. Add cocoa powder, almond milk, sweetener, vanilla extract, and a pinch of salt.
3. Blend until smooth and creamy. Taste and adjust sweetness if necessary.
4. Spoon into serving dishes and refrigerate for 5 minutes to thicken.
5. Garnish with fresh berries and whipped cream if desired.

Nutritional value:
- Calories: 120 kcal
- Protein: 2g
- Carbs: 6g
- Fiber: 4g
- Fat: 11g

NO-BAKE PEANUT BUTTER BARS
SERVINGS: 2   🕒 15 MINUTES

Ingredients
- 1 cup peanut butter
- 1/4 cup honey
- 1/2 cup rolled oats
- 1/4 cup chocolate chips (melted)

Instruction
1. Mix peanut butter, honey, and rolled oats until well combined.
2. Press the mixture into an 8x8 inch pan.
3. Drizzle melted chocolate chips on top.
4. Refrigerate for 30 minutes, then cut into bars.

Nutritional value:
- 250 calories per bar
- Protein: 8g
- Carbs: 30g
- Fat: 12g

Dinner

CHEESECAKE BITES
SERVINGS: 12 bites 🕒 40 MINUTES

Ingredients

- 8 oz cream cheese, softened
- 1/4 cup powdered erythritol (or other keto sweetener)
- 1 tsp vanilla extract
- 1/2 cup heavy cream
- Fresh berries or chocolate shavings for garnish

Instruction

1. In a mixing bowl, beat cream cheese until smooth.
2. Add powdered erythritol and vanilla extract, mixing until well combined.
3. In another bowl, whip heavy cream until stiff peaks form.
4. Gently fold whipped cream into the cream cheese mixture until smooth.
5. Spoon mixture into a mini-muffin pan or silicone molds and refrigerate for 1 hour.
6. Serve topped with berries or chocolate shavings.

Nutritional value:

- Calories: 80 kcal
- Protein: 1g
- Carbs: 1g
- Fiber: 0g
- Fat: 7g

APPLE NACHOS
SERVINGS: 2 serving 🕒 30 MINUTES

Ingredients

- 2 apples, thinly sliced
- 2 tbsp peanut butter (melted)
- 2 tbsp chocolate chips
- 2 tbsp shredded coconut
- 1 tbsp chopped nuts

Instruction

1. Arrange apple slices on a plate.
2. Drizzle melted peanut butter over the apples.
3. Sprinkle chocolate chips, shredded coconut, and chopped nuts.

Nutritional value:

- 180 calories per serving
- Protein: 2g
- Carbs: 35g
- Fat: 6g

Small bite

KETO CUPCAKES
SERVINGS: 8 cupcakes   🕒 30 MINUTES

Ingredients

- 8 cupcakes
- Ingredients
- 1 cup almond flour
- 1/4 cup unsweetened cocoa powder
- 1/4 cup erythritol
- 1 tsp baking powder
- 3 large eggs
- 1/4 cup coconut oil, melted
- 1/4 cup almond milk
- 1 tsp vanilla extract

Instruction

1. Preheat the oven to 350°F (175°C). Line a muffin tin with cupcake liners.
2. In a large bowl, mix almond flour, cocoa powder, erythritol, baking powder, and salt.
3. In a separate bowl, whisk together eggs, melted coconut oil, almond milk, and vanilla extract.
4. Add the wet ingredients to the dry ingredients and stir until well combined.
5. Pour the batter into the cupcake liners, filling each about 3/4 full.
6. Bake for 20-25 minutes or until a toothpick inserted into the center comes out clean.
7. Cool before serving.

Nutritional value:

- Calories: 150 kcal
- Protein: 5g
- Carbs: 4g
- Fat: 12g

MICROWAVE S'MORES
SERVINGS: 1 serving   🕒 25 MINUTES

Ingredients

- 2 graham crackers
- 1 large marshmallow
- 1 piece of chocolate (about 1 inch)

Instruction

1. Place a piece of chocolate on a graham cracker.
2. Top with a marshmallow and microwave for 10-15 seconds.
3. Press the second graham cracker on top to create a sandwich.

Nutritional value:

- 150 calories per serving
- Protein: 2g
- Carbs: 25g
- Fat: 5g

Lunch

ALMOND FLOUR COOKIES
SERVINGS: 12 cookies ⏱ 30 MINUTES

Ingredients

- 12 cookies
- Ingredients
- 2 cups almond flour
- 1/4 cup coconut oil or butter, melted
- 1/4 cup erythritol
- 1 tsp vanilla extract
- 1/4 tsp salt
- Optional: 1/4 cup sugar-free chocolate chips

Instruction

1. Preheat the oven to 350°F (175°C) and line a baking sheet with parchment paper.
2. In a large bowl, mix almond flour, erythritol, and salt.
3. Add melted coconut oil (or butter) and vanilla extract, stirring until a dough forms.
4. Fold in chocolate chips if desired.
5. Scoop out 1 tbsp of dough and shape into balls, placing them on the baking sheet. Flatten slightly.
6. Bake for 12-15 minutes until golden brown around the edges.
7. Cool on a wire rack.

Nutritional value:

- Calories: 100 kcal
- Protein: 3g
- Carbs: 2g
- Fiber: 1g
- Fat: 8g

CARAMEL POPCORN
SERVINGS: 4 serving ⏱ 10 MINUTES

Ingredients

- 6 cups popcorn (air-popped)
- 1/2 cup brown sugar
- 1/4 cup butter
- 2 tbsp corn syrup
- 1/4 tsp baking soda
- 1/4 tsp vanilla extract

Instruction

1. In a saucepan, melt butter, brown sugar, and corn syrup over medium heat.
2. Bring to a boil, then remove from heat and stir in baking soda and vanilla.
3. Pour caramel over popcorn and mix well.
4. Let cool before serving.

Nutritional value:

- 150 calories per serving
- Protein: 2g
- Carbs: 20g
- Fat: 7g

Lunch

KETO ICE CREAM
SERVINGS: 4   🕒 30 MINUTES

Ingredients
- 1 cup heavy cream
- 1/2 cup unsweetened almond milk
- 1/4 cup erythritol
- 1 tsp vanilla extract
- Optional: 1/4 cup sugar-free chocolate chips

Instruction
1. In a bowl, whisk together heavy cream, almond milk, erythritol, and vanilla extract.
2. Pour the mixture into an ice cream maker and churn according to the manufacturer's instructions. Alternatively, pour into a container and freeze, stirring every 30 minutes until desired consistency.
3. Add chocolate chips during the last few minutes of churning or stirring.
4. Serve immediately or freeze until firm.

Nutritional value:
- Calories: 160 kcal
- Protein: 2g
- Carbs: 3g
- Fiber: 0g
- Fat: 16g

COCONUT MACAROONS
SERVINGS: 12 macaroons   🕒 15 MINUTES

Ingredients
- 2 1/2 cups shredded sweetened coconut
- 2/3 cup sweetened condensed milk
- 1 tsp vanilla extract
- 2 large egg whites
- Pinch of salt

Instruction
1. Preheat oven to 325°F (160°C). Line a baking sheet with parchment paper.
2. In a bowl, mix shredded coconut, sweetened condensed milk, and vanilla extract.
3. In a separate bowl, beat egg whites with a pinch of salt until stiff peaks form.
4. Fold the egg whites into the coconut mixture.
5. Drop spoonful's of the mixture onto the baking sheet.
6. Bake for 15 minutes or until golden brown.

Nutritional value:
- 110 calories per macaroon
- Protein: 2g
- Carbs: 12g
- Fat: 6g

Lunch

COCONUT CHIA PUDDING
SERVINGS: 8 cupcakes   🕒 60 minutes

Ingredients
- 1 cup unsweetened coconut milk
- 2 tbsp chia seeds
- 1 tbsp erythritol or keto sweetener of choice
- 1/2 tsp vanilla extract
- Optional toppings: shredded coconut, fresh berries, or chopped nuts

Instruction
1. In a bowl, whisk together coconut milk, chia seeds, erythritol, and vanilla extract.
2. Let the mixture sit for 5 minutes, then whisk again to prevent clumping.
3. Cover and refrigerate for at least 4 hours or overnight until it reaches a thick, pudding-like consistency.
4. Serve chilled, topped with shredded coconut, berries, or nuts if desired.

Nutritional value:
- Calories: 120 kcal
- Protein: 2g
- Carbs: 4g
- Fiber: 3g
- Fat: 10g

NUTELLA BANANA ROLL-UPS
SERVINGS: 2   🕒 5 minutes

Ingredients
- 2 flour tortillas
- 2 tbsp Nutella
- 1 ripe banana, sliced
- 1 tsp honey (optional)

Instruction
1. Lay out each tortilla and spread 1 tablespoon of Nutella evenly.
2. Place banana slices evenly over the Nutella.
3. Drizzle with honey if desired.
4. Roll up tightly and slice into bite-sized pieces.

Nutritional value:
- 180 calories per serving
- Protein: 4g
- Carbs: 26g
- Fat: 8g

Breakfast

VANILLA BEAN PANNA COTTA
SERVINGS: 4 🕐 30 MINUTES

Ingredients
- 1 cup heavy cream
- 1/2 cup unsweetened almond milk
- 2 tbsp erythritol or sweetener of choice
- 1 tsp vanilla extract or 1/2 vanilla bean (seeds scraped)
- 1/2 tbsp unflavored gelatin powder
- 1 tbsp cold water
- Optional: fresh berries for garnish

Instruction
1. In a small bowl, sprinkle gelatin over cold water and let it bloom for 5 minutes.
2. In a saucepan, combine heavy cream, almond milk, and erythritol. Heat over medium, stirring until erythritol dissolves.
3. Add vanilla extract (or vanilla bean seeds) and the gelatin mixture to the saucepan, whisking until gelatin fully dissolves.
4. Pour mixture into small serving dishes and refrigerate for at least 4 hours or until set.
5. Serve with fresh berries if desired.

Nutritional value:
- Calories: 120 kcal
- Protein: 2g
- Carbs: 4g
- Fat: 10g

CINNAMON APPLE CRUMBLE
SERVINGS: 4 🕐 15 MINUTES

Ingredients
- 2 large apples, peeled and diced
- 2 tbsp butter
- 1/4 cup brown sugar
- 1/2 tsp cinnamon
- 1/4 cup rolled oats
- 1/4 cup all-purpose flour
- 2 tbsp melted butter

Instruction
1. Preheat oven to 350°F (175°C). Grease a small baking dish.
2. In a skillet, cook diced apples with 2 tablespoons butter, brown sugar, and cinnamon for 5 minutes until soft.
3. In a separate bowl, mix oats, flour, and melted butter until crumbly.
4. Pour the cooked apples into the baking dish and sprinkle the crumble mixture over the top.
5. Bake for 10 minutes or until golden brown.

Nutritional value:
- 220 calories per serving
- Protein: 2g
- Carbs: 40g
- Fat: 8g

Dinner

CHAPTER SIX: BUILDING YOUR KETO PANTRY: ESSENTIAL STAPLES FOR A LOW-CARB LIFESTYLE

KETO PANTRY LIST - ESSENTIAL KETO-FRIENDLY STAPLES

A well-stocked keto pantry ensures you're always ready to make delicious, low-carb meals. Here's a guide to key keto-friendly staples:

Oils & Fats

- **Coconut Oil:** Great for high-heat cooking and rich in MCTs (medium-chain triglycerides).
- **Olive Oil:** Ideal for dressings and medium-heat cooking; high in monounsaturated fats.
- **Avocado Oil**: Excellent for all types of cooking; high in healthy fats.
- **Ghee/Butter:** Adds flavor and fat; great for cooking, baking, and spreading.

Low-Carb Flours

- **Almond Flour:** Versatile for baking and breading.
- **Coconut Flour:** Absorbs more liquid; use in small amounts.
- **Flaxseed Meal:** Adds fiber and can act as an egg substitute.

Sweeteners

- **Erythritol:** Zero-calorie, low-glycemic sweetener; resembles sugar in texture.
- **Stevia:** Natural, highly concentrated sweetener; pairs well with erythritol.
- **Monk Fruit Sweetener:** Natural, no-calorie sweetener with a similar taste to sugar.
- **Allulose:** Tastes like sugar and works well in baking.

Nutritional Facts

- **Oils (per tbsp):** 120 calories, 14g fat, 0g carbs, 0g protein.
- **Almond Flour (1/4 cup):** 160 calories, 14g fat, 3g net carbs, 6g protein.
- **Erythritol (per tsp):** 0 calories, 0g fat, 0g carbs (non-glycemic), 0g protein.

BEST FRESH FOODS FOR KETO

Choose low-carb, high-fat foods to stay within keto guidelines. These options help simplify choices with visual guides like charts.

Vegetables

- **Leafy Greens:** Spinach, kale, arugula.
- **Cruciferous Veggies:** Broccoli, cauliflower, Brussels sprouts.
- **Low-Carb Options:** Zucchini, cucumber, bell peppers.

Proteins

- **Meat:** Beef, chicken, lamb, pork (focus on fatty cuts).
- **Seafood:** Salmon, sardines, shrimp (rich in omega-3).
- **Eggs:** A versatile, nutrient-dense choice.

Healthy Fats

- **Avocados:** Rich in healthy fats and potassium.
- **Nuts & Seeds:** Almonds, chia seeds, flaxseeds.
- Cheese & Dairy: Cheddar, mozzarella, Greek yogurt (full-fat).

INGREDIENT SUBSTITUTIONS FOR KETO COOKING

Replacing high-carb ingredients can make traditional dishes keto-friendly. Here are some helpful swaps:

- **Wheat Flour** → Almond/Coconut Flour: Almond flour has 2g net carbs per 1/4 cup, while coconut flour has 2g net carbs per tbsp.
- **Sugar** → Erythritol/Monk Fruit: Both are low-glycemic, calorie-free sweeteners.
- **Pasta/Rice** → Zoodles/Cauliflower Rice: Low-carb veggie replacements for common high-carb sides.
- **Breadcrumbs** → Pork Rind Crumbs/Almond Flour: Pork rinds offer a similar crunch without the carbs.

30 DAYS MEAL PLAN

The plan focuses on high-fat, moderate protein, and very low carbs, all designed to keep you in ketosis.

Day 1

Breakfast: Keto Avocado and Egg Bowl - 1 avocado halved with 2 fried eggs, bacon bits, and fresh herbs.
Lunch: Cobb Salad - Grilled chicken, bacon, avocado, hard-boiled egg, and blue cheese over mixed greens.
Dinner: Garlic Butter Steak Bites with Zucchini Noodles.
Snack: Cheese sticks or olives.

Day 2

Breakfast: Keto Smoothie - Almond milk, spinach, avocado, chia seeds, and a scoop of protein powder.
Lunch: Tuna Salad Lettuce Wraps with celery, mayo, and dill.
Dinner: Baked Salmon with a side of roasted asparagus in olive oil.
Snack: 10-12 Almonds.

Day 3

Breakfast: Scrambled Eggs with Cheese, spinach, and mushrooms cooked in butter.
Lunch: Grilled Chicken Caesar Salad - Romaine, chicken breast, Caesar dressing, and Parmesan cheese.
Dinner: Keto Meatloaf with a side of mashed cauliflower.
Snack: A handful of macadamia nuts.

Day 4

Breakfast: Chia Seed Pudding - Coconut milk, chia seeds, and a few berries.
Lunch: Zucchini Boats stuffed with cream cheese, cheddar, and ground beef.
Dinner: Chicken Thighs in Creamy Garlic Sauce with sautéed green beans.
Snack: ¼ cup guacamole with celery sticks.

Day 5

Breakfast: Keto Pancakes with almond flour, served with sugar-free syrup and butter.
Lunch: Egg Salad with Mayo and Dijon Mustard on a bed of mixed greens.
Dinner: Grilled Pork Chops with a side of roasted Brussels sprouts.
Snack: 1 ounce of dark chocolate (85% cacao).

Day 6

- **Breakfast:** Bacon and Spinach Omelette with cheese.
- **Lunch:** Avocado Chicken Salad with cilantro, lime, and a side of fresh salad greens.
- **Dinner:** Keto Chicken Parmesan - Chicken breasts with marinara sauce and mozzarella cheese, served with a side salad.
- **Snack:** 1-2 slices of salami with cream cheese.

Day 7

- **Breakfast:** Bulletproof Coffee (coffee blended with 1 tbsp of grass-fed butter and 1 tbsp of MCT oil or coconut oil).
- **Lunch:** Cheeseburger Salad - Ground beef, cheddar, pickles, tomato, and keto-friendly dressing over romaine.
- **Dinner:** Shrimp Scampi over zucchini noodles.
- **Snack:** Small handful of walnuts.

Day 8

- **Breakfast:** Keto Breakfast Casserole - Eggs, sausage, bell peppers, and cheddar cheese.
- **Lunch:** Broccoli and Cheese Soup.
- **Dinner:** Baked Chicken Wings with a side of cauliflower rice.
- **Snack:** Pepperoni slices with cheese.

Day 9

- **Breakfast:** Greek Yogurt (unsweetened) with chia seeds, a few raspberries, and a splash of vanilla extract.
- **Lunch:** Caprese Salad with mozzarella, tomato, basil, and balsamic vinegar.
- **Dinner:** Ribeye Steak with garlic butter and roasted broccoli.
- **Snack:** Handful of pecans.

Day 10

- **Breakfast:** Cottage Cheese with a few slices of cucumber and a drizzle of olive oil.
- **Lunch:** BLT Lettuce Wraps - Bacon, lettuce, tomato, and mayo wrapped in lettuce leaves.
- **Dinner:** Ground Turkey Stuffed Peppers with cheese.
- **Snack:** Deviled Eggs.

Day 11

- **Breakfast:** Keto Sausage Egg Muffins.
- **Lunch:** Tuna Melt on Portobello mushrooms.
- **Dinner:** Pork Tenderloin with a side of sautéed spinach.
- **Snack:** Cheese crisps.

Day 12

- **Breakfast:** Scrambled Eggs with Avocado and salsa.
- **Lunch:** Leftover Chicken Thighs with a fresh side salad.
- **Dinner:** Lemon Butter Cod with a side of sautéed zucchini.
- **Snack:** A handful of sunflower seeds.

Day 13

- **Breakfast:** Flaxseed Keto Granola with almond milk.
- **Lunch:** Ham and Swiss Roll-ups with mustard and pickles.
- **Dinner:** Beef Stir Fry with bell peppers and sesame oil (low-carb soy sauce).
- **Snack:** Pork rinds with a dip.

Day 14

- **Breakfast:** Keto Breakfast Burrito - scrambled eggs, sausage, cheese, and avocado wrapped in a low-carb tortilla.
- **Lunch:** Spinach Salad with feta, bacon, and a boiled egg.
- **Dinner:** Baked Italian Meatballs in marinara sauce with a side of zucchini noodles.
- **Snack:** Half an avocado with salt and pepper.

Day 15

- **Breakfast:** Almond Flour Waffles with sugar-free syrup.
- **Lunch:** Chicken Caesar Lettuce Wraps.
- **Dinner:** Grilled Lamb Chops with garlic butter and a side of Greek salad.
- **Snack:** Cucumber slices with cream cheese.

Day 16

- **Breakfast:** Hard-boiled Eggs with a side of smoked salmon.
- **Lunch:** Keto Taco Salad - Ground beef, cheese, avocado, sour cream, and salsa.
- **Dinner:** Keto Alfredo with shirataki noodles.
- **Snack:** Almond butter on celery sticks.

Day 17

- **Breakfast:** Fried Eggs with sautéed mushrooms and bell peppers.
- **Lunch:** Leftover Meatballs with a side of green salad.
- **Dinner:** Baked Cod with lemon and butter, served with a side of roasted veggies.
- **Snack:** Keto Fat Bombs (cream cheese, cocoa powder, and coconut oil).

Day 18

- **Breakfast:** Keto Avocado Toast on a slice of low-carb bread.
- **Lunch**: Turkey Club Salad - Turkey, bacon, avocado, tomato, and ranch dressing.
- **Dinner:** Chicken Alfredo Casserole.
- **Snack:** String cheese.

Day 19

- **Breakfast:** Spinach and Cheese Omelette.
- **Lunch**: Shrimp Caesar Salad with extra Parmesan.
- **Dinner**: Pork Carnitas with a side of cauliflower rice.
- **Snack:** Mixed nuts (avoid cashews).

Day 20

- **Breakfast:** Keto Egg Muffins with cheese, ham, and spinach.
- **Lunch**: Beef and Broccoli Stir Fry.
- **Dinner:** Keto Shepherd's Pie with cauliflower mash topping.
- **Snack:** 2-3 slices of smoked sausage.

Day 21

- **Breakfast:** Sausage and Cheese Breakfast Casserole.
- **Lunch:** Leftover Pork Carnitas with a side of fresh salad greens.
- **Dinner**: Seared Scallops with garlic butter, served with sautéed spinach.
- **Snack:** Keto mug cake.

Day 22

- **Breakfast**: Keto Chaffles (cheese waffles) with cream cheese and smoked salmon.
- **Lunch:** Chicken Salad with celery, mayo, and Dijon mustard.
- **Dinner:** Grilled Salmon with a side of Greek salad.
- **Snack:** Olives and a slice of cheese.

Day 23

- **Breakfast**: Keto French Toast with a side of bacon.
- **Lunch:** Egg Drop Soup with extra spinach.
- **Dinner**: Beef Stroganoff with zucchini noodles.
- **Snack:** Keto Trail Mix (nuts, seeds, coconut flakes).

Day 24

- **Breakfast:** Keto Cinnamon Roll in a Mug.
- **Lunch:** Antipasto Salad with salami, mozzarella, olives, and greens.
- **Dinner:** Lemon Herb Chicken Thighs with roasted Brussels sprouts.
- **Snack:** Keto fat bomb.

Day 25

- **Breakfast:** Bacon, Egg, and Cheese Cups (baked in a muffin tin).
- **Lunch:** Grilled Shrimp Salad with avocado and a citrus vinaigrette.
- **Dinner:** Stuffed Bell Peppers with cheese and ground beef.
- **Snack:** ¼ cup of full-fat cottage cheese.

Day 26

- **Breakfast:** Keto Oatmeal (flax, chia seeds, almond milk).
- **Lunch:** Keto Pizza - Low-carb crust with cheese, pepperoni, and veggies.
- **Dinner:** Baked Chicken Breasts with mushroom cream sauce.
- **Snack:** Pickles with a side of cheese.

Day 27

- **Breakfast:** Eggs Benedict with Hollandaise Sauce on a slice of tomato or low-carb toast.
- **Lunch:** Roast Beef Lettuce Wraps with cheese and mustard.
- **Dinner:** Garlic Shrimp with a side of sautéed zucchini.
- **Snack:** Half a bell pepper with ranch dip.

Day 28

- **Breakfast:** Keto Bagels with cream cheese.
- **Lunch:** Caprese Chicken - Grilled chicken with mozzarella, basil, and tomato.
- **Dinner:** Spaghetti Squash Alfredo with grilled chicken.
- **Snack:** Almond butter.

Day 29

- **Breakfast:** Keto Blueberry Muffins.
- **Lunch:** Greek Salad with grilled chicken.
- **Dinner:** Ribeye with creamed spinach.
- **Snack:** Seaweed snacks.

Day 30

- **Breakfast:** Keto Hash - Turnips, sausage, eggs, and cheese.
- **Lunch:** Avocado Tuna Salad.
- **Dinner:** Grilled Chicken Drumsticks with roasted cauliflower.
- **Snack:** Handful of pecans.

SHOPPING LIST

PROTEIN SOURCES

Meat & Poultry:
- Beef (steak, ground beef, roasts)
- Pork (bacon, pork chops, sausage without added sugar)
- Chicken (thighs, wings, breast)
- Turkey
- Lamb
- Veal

Fish & Seafood:
- Salmon
- Tuna
- Mackerel
- Sardines
- Shrimp
- Crab
- Cod
- Halibut

Eggs:
- Large eggs (organic or free-range if possible)
- Egg whites (for recipes if needed)

HEALTHY FATS & OILS

Cooking Oils:
- Olive oil (extra virgin)
- Coconut oil
- Avocado oil
- Ghee or clarified butter
- Grass-fed butter
- MCT oil

Other Fats:
- Lard
- Tallow
- Duck fat

DAIRY (OPTIONAL IF YOU TOLERATE IT)
- Heavy whipping cream
- Full-fat sour cream
- Cream cheese
- Greek yogurt (full-fat, unsweetened)
- Hard cheeses (cheddar, parmesan, gouda)
- Soft cheeses (brie, camembert)
- Cottage cheese (full-fat)
- Mozzarella

LOW-CARB VEGETABLES

Leafy Greens:
- Spinach
- Kale
- Arugula
- Romaine lettuce
- Swiss chard
- Collard greens

Cruciferous Vegetables:
- Broccoli
- Cauliflower
- Brussels sprouts
- Cabbage
- Bok choy

Other Low-Carb Veggies:
- Zucchini
- Bell peppers (especially green)
- Avocado
- Asparagus
- Cucumber
- Celery
- Mushrooms
- Green beans

NUTS & SEEDS
- Almonds
- Walnuts
- Pecans
- Macadamia nuts
- Brazil nuts
- Hazelnuts
- Chia seeds

BAKING & PANTRY ESSENTIALS
- Almond flour
- Coconut flour
- Psyllium husk
- Baking powder
- Unsweetened cocoa powder

FROZEN FOODS
- Frozen berries (raspberries, blackberries, strawberries - use sparingly)
- Frozen spinach, broccoli, or other low-carb veggies
- Frozen cauliflower rice
- Frozen shrimp or other seafood

Keto Diet Metric Conversion Chart

Basic Volume Conversions
U.S. Measurement
Metric Equivalent

U.S. Measurement Metric Equivalent

U.S. Measurement	Metric Equivalent
1 ounce (oz)	28 grams (g)
4 ounces	113 grams (g)
8 ounces	227 grams (g)
12 ounces	340 grams (g)
1 pound (lb)	454 grams (g)

Nut Flours and Sweeteners (Volume to Weight)

Ingredient	U.S Measurement	Metric Weight
Almond Flour	1 Cup	96 grams (g)
Coconut Flour	1 cup	112 grams (g)
Erythritol	1 cup	200 grams (g)
Monk Fruit Sweetener	1 cup	190 grams (g)

U.S. Measurement Metric Equivalent

U.S. Measurement	Metric Equivalent
1 teaspoon (tsp)	5 milliliters (ml)
1 tablespoon (tbsp)	15 milliliters (ml)
1/4 cup	60 milliliters (ml)
1/3 cup	80 milliliters (ml)
1/2 cup	120 milliliters (ml)
2/3 cup	160 milliliters (ml)
3/4 cup	180 milliliters (ml)
1 cup	240 milliliters (ml)

Common Oils and Fats (Volume to Weight)

Ingredient	U.S. Measurement	Metric Weight
Coconut Oil	1 tablespoon	14 grams (g)
Butter	1 tablespoon	14 grams (g)
Olive Oil	1 tablespoon	13 grams (g)

Temperature Conversions

Fahrenheit (°F)	Celsius (°C)
200°F	93°C
250°F	121°C
300°F	149°C
350°F	177°C
400°F	204°C
450°F	232°C

Congratulations on completing your journey through this keto cookbook! I hope these recipes inspire you to embrace a healthier lifestyle without sacrificing flavor or variety. Whether you're just starting out or are a seasoned keto enthusiast, remember that every meal is a step toward your goals. Celebrate the small victories, explore new flavors, and keep experimenting in your kitchen—your journey to better health is uniquely yours.

This book was made with love, passion, and a deep commitment to helping you succeed. If you've enjoyed the recipes or found them helpful, I'd be delighted to hear your story. Share your experience, connect with others, and keep building a community that celebrates good food and better health.

As you close this book, take with you not only the recipes but also the confidence to create meals that nourish your body and soul. The ketogenic lifestyle isn't just a diet—it's a way of rediscovering the joy of mindful eating, the power of fresh ingredients, and the strength within yourself to prioritize wellness.

Thank you for inviting me into your kitchen and allowing me to be part of your keto adventure. This is just the beginning of your journey—keep exploring, keep cooking, and most importantly, keep thriving. Here's to more delicious moments, one low-carb bite at a time!

With   gratitude,
Mario Pacino

Thank you for diving into these keto recipes with me! I truly hope this collection of keto recipes has brought inspiration and ease to your lifestyle! Your feedback is invaluable, so if you've enjoyed this book, I would be so grateful if you could **leave a review** *to share your thoughts and encourage others to embrace the keto lifestyle.*

Printed in Great Britain
by Amazon